SELECTED PLAYS OF GUAN HANQING

TRANSLATED BY YANG XIANYI AND GLADYS YANG

Selected Plays of Guan Hanqing

Translated by Yang Xianyi and Gladys Yang

Copyright 2007 Silk Pagoda

ISBN: 1-59654-390-6

Silk Pagoda is an imprint of

Disruptive Publishing

TABLE OF CONTENTS

FOREWORD 5

SNOW IN MIDSUMMER 17

THE WIFE-SNATCHER.. 53

THE BUTTERFLY DREAM 99

RESCUED BY A COQUETTE... 139

THE RIVERSIDE PAVILION 173

THE JADE MIRROR-STAND.. 209

LORD GUAN GOES TO THE FEAST 247

DEATH OF THE WINGED-TIGER GENERAL 285

FOREWORD

Wang Jisi[1]

The Chinese feudal economy reached a high stage of development in the eleventh century during the Northern Song Dynasty, when handicraft industries and commerce flourished and the urban class gained in strength. As printing was by now in general use, the craftsmen and tradesmen in the cities were able to read popular *chante-fables* or the librettos of operas, and this was a fruitful time for story-telling and the theatre. In Bianliang, present-day Kaifeng, the capital of the Northern Song Dynasty, gathered all manner of folk artists who sang, told stories and put on variety shows, including simple comic operas.

In 1126, the Nuchen Tartars from the north-east established the Kingdom of Jin in northern China, and the Song emperor was forced to move to Hangzhou south of the Chang Jiang (Yangtze) River, which became the capital of the Southern Song Dynasty. During the years when the country was divided, the northern Chinese absorbed into their own music the more stirring melodies of the Nuchen Tartars, who sang on horseback to the accompaniment of fiddles. So came into being a new northern school of music. The music popular at this time in the south was softer and more euphonious—a chamber music suitable for performance during feasts.

In 1234, the Mongols from the desert regions north of the Great Wall, led by Genghis Khan's son Ogutai, overthrew the Kingdom of Jin. In 1279, Genghis Khan's grandson Kublai Khan overthrew the Southern Song empire, uniting all China once more and founding the Yuan Dynasty.

Political conditions under the Mongols were among the worst in Chinese history. Because the people suffered untold hardships yet fought resolutely against their corrupt and despotic

---

[1] Professor of the Department of Chinese Literature in Sun Yat-sen University, Guangzhou.

rulers, the literature of that period—the drama in particular—breathes a strong fighting spirit. On the whole, the vigorous northern tunes were best suited to express the prevalent mood; thus most of the melodies in the Yuan drama come from the northern music. A type of dramatic ballad popular among townsfolk and known as the *zhu-gong-diao* also had a great influence on the Yuan theatre. Such ballads were usually performed by a woman with a clapper in her hand, who reinforced her recitation and songs with simple actions and gestures accompanied by music. This was in fact an early form of drama.

A Yuan play is usually divided into four acts, which present the problem, build it up, bring it to a climax and provide a denouement. Sometimes in addition to these four acts a short scene was inserted to introduce minor episodes. When the action was too involved to be contained in four acts, more acts were added, as in the case of the famous drama *Romance of the West Chamber*. A play seldom had more than one leading male or female character. Thus Guan Hanqing's *Snow in Midsummer* and *Rescued by a Coquette* have a heroine in the main role, while all the other characters merely speak instead of singing—a relic of the dramatic ballad related by a single performer.

Intellectuals in feudal China tried to gain official posts by passing the government examinations. Since there were always many unsuccessful candidates, during the eleventh and twelfth centuries educated men who had failed in the examinations often attached themselves to the entertainment parks then popular in the large cities and wrote for the townsfolk, sometimes even taking part themselves in plays or variety shows. When the Mongols abolished the examination system which had opened the way to an official career for feudal intellectuals, many scholars were left without a profession and went down in the social scale. China was now united; there were good communications by land and sea within the empire and with countries to the west, and a prosperous mercantile economy in such cities as Cambaluc (present-day Beijing), Kaifeng and Hangzhou; so the popular arts were in ever greater demand. This provided new opportunities for the intellectuals, many of whom co-operated with actors and storytellers, writing librettos or ballads for them. The townsfolk called such scholars "talented men." They had their own guilds or "book societies," in which they worked, exchanged experience and sometimes held dramatic contests. Indeed the appearance of these professional guilds gave fresh impetus to the development of the theatre. The brilliant playwright Guan Hanqing, one of the great names of Chinese literature, was undoubtedly—judging by historical records and what remains of his work—the most outstanding dramatist among the "talented men" of the Yuan Dynasty.

After overthrowing the Kingdom of Jin, the Mongols in 1264 set up their capital in Cambaluc. In 1279, after the overthrow of the Southern Song Dynasty, Cambaluc became the political and economic centre of the whole of China. Some famous writers in the north founded the Yu-jing Book Society there, and Guan Hanqing was one of its most active members. In his youth he had been a keen student and learned to write all forms of poetry and song. He soon became well-known in the capital for his versatility, his strong sense of humour, remarkable proficiency in music, dancing and singing, and his skill in the football game then in vogue.

From the middle of the thirteenth century to the beginning of the fourteenth was the great age of Yuan drama, when many playwrights of note were assembled in the capital. While there, Guan Hanqing formed his own company of players and sometimes trod the boards himself. Thus he knew every aspect of the theatre.

Between the eleventh and thirteenth centuries all the singing in ballads and operas in the entertainment parks was done by singsong girls, most of whom had been sold to brothels by bankrupt parents, although a few were sent there because their families had opposed the government. Theirs was the lowest place in the social order, and such were their humiliation and hardships that they conceived an intense hatred for the rich and mighty. Guan Hanqing was one of the "talented men" who remained in close touch with these singsong girls as. well as with other members of the lowest walks of life during his career as playwright and actor. Knowing them so well, he came to sympathize with them and respect them. Through them he familiarized himself with the techniques of folk art and the vivid expressions of urban speech. This knowledge enabled him to show the sterling qualities and magnificent courage of Chinese womanhood in his plays, to present a comprehensive and truthful picture of town life, and to bring out the genuine nobility of humble folk.

We do not know the exact date of Guan Hanqing's birth and death. Judging by certain records of his time, he was born in the twenties or thirties of the thirteenth century and died at the end of it. Most of his plays were written in the later half of the century, especially in the last two decades—the heyday of the theatre in Cambaluc.

Guan Hanqing was one of the most prolific of the Yuan Dynasty dramatists. Titles of more than sixty of his works are known today, and eighteen of these are still extant. This volume contains a selection of eight of these plays.

Snow in Midsummer, The Wife-Snatcher and *The Butterfly Dream* deal mainly with justice and trials. *Rescued by a Coquette, The Riverside Pavilion* and *The Jade Mirror-Stand* have love and marriage as their themes. *Lord Guan Goes to the Feast* and *Death of the Winged-Tiger General* are historical plays.

Of the first group, *Snow in Midsummer* makes the greatest emotional appeal. Dou E's struggle with the Zhangs and the prefect is a penetrating exposure of the corrupt state of local politics and the social disorder during the Yuan Dynasty, while her rebellious spirit symbolizes the determined resistance of the common people to their cruel oppressors.

The law at that time decreed that the highest officials in the local government must be Mongols or other Tartars—who knew little about regional conditions. As much power was in the hands of their Han deputies, the local authorities were venal and the backward forces of feudalism were unchecked. Dou E loses her mother when she is three, and at seven is sold by her father to the Cai family as a child-bride. She marries at seventeen, but the next year her husband dies, leaving her alone with her mother-in-law. Naturally in such a society these two widows are insulted and abused. But a brave people never gives in. Just before her execution, Dou E swears that after her death Heaven will send down snow in midsummer. The dramatist uses this folk legend to bring out the girl's defiance to authority and her fighting tenacity—a tenacity which moves heaven and earth and persists even after her death. This is a vivid reflection of the essence of that society: the indomitable will of the people and their stubborn opposition to the powers of darkness. It is a characteristic of Chinese tragedy that popular heroes and heroines will not lay down their arms even as ghosts.

Mistress Wang in *The Butterfly Dream*, who lets her own son die rather than give up the sons of her husband's first wife, is the good mother of traditional Chinese morality. It goes without saying that she loves her son, and she offers to die in his place; but when the judge insists that one of the young men must lose his life, she sacrifices her own boy. After the release of her two stepsons she starts to mourn for her own child. But when they mourn for him too, she comforts them by saying that since they are spared she is content. This is a truthful picture of the mixed emotions of this common woman who, despite the heavy blows she suffers, displays such remarkable fortitude and powers of endurance.

She, too, has no respect for wealth and rank. When a noble kills her husband, she demands that he be tried in the same way as an ordinary citizen. When Prefect Bao wants to execute her stepsons for avenging their father, she clings to their cangues and calls the judge a fool. And when finally she has to let her own son go to his death, she tells him that once he meets his dead father in the shades they must hurl the murderer down into hell.

The Wife-Snatcher shows the tragedy of the families broken up by oppressive rule. At that time the troops stationed by the Mongols in different parts of the country abducted women and seized property at will. Lu Zhailang in this play is such a character. But as the playwright could not speak out directly against such iniquities, he had to present this as a story of a previous dynasty.

The second act, describing how Zhang Gui is forced to take his wife to Lu Zhailang's house, contains one of the most realistic passages in our classical drama. Since Lu is so powerful, Zhang has to deliver his wife to him at dawn. But unable to explain this to his wife, he pretends that he is taking her to a relative's wedding. Upon reaching Lu's house, he tries to drown his sorrows in wine; and his wife, not realizing that they are to part, urges him not to drink so much. Then Zhang bursts out with the truth, and she reproaches him. By means of such telling details, Guan Hanqing brings home vividly to his audiences the love between the husband and wife, their happiness and impending disaster.

Both in *The Wife-Snatcher* and *The Butterfly Dream,* the official who champions the common people is Prefect Bao, a historical figure. Bao Zheng was a fair and just official of the eleventh century. Because so few feudal functionaries had any sense of justice, stories about this good official spread and he became virtually deified. During the Yuan Dynasty, the general resentment against the government and longing for better rule made plays about Prefect Bao more popular than ever.

The three plays in this selection about love and various comedies of errors are among the best Yuan Dynasty dramas of this type.

The Jade Mirror-Stand is based on a traditional story about an old husband with a young wife. Though such a marriage is unnatural, Guan Hanqing approved of it because in his time polygamy was allowed; and since one husband could have many wives, it was better for a woman to marry an older man who was devoted to her than a young one with divided affections. The author's view was conditioned by his times. From the advice which Wen gives his wife, we can see how rich young men treated their wives and the loneliness of the unfortunate women who were forsaken—a common enough occurrence when a man had many concubines.

The Riverside Pavilion is packed with suspense and surprises from the first act when the abbess tricks Tan Jier into marrying her nephew, to the last when Tan Jier confronts Lord Yang. The third act is particularly good theatre, when the heroine approaches the enemy in disguise, catches them off their guard and disarms them. Her courage and tact are contrasted with the worthlessness and weakness of the seemingly mighty Lord Yang.

Tan Jier is a widow, and according to feudal conventions she should not remarry; but Guan Hanqing evidently considers it right for her to marry a second husband who respects her. This was an advanced view for those times, and a strongly anti-feudal one, for it meant considering the problem of second marriage for a widow not from the standpoint of feudal morality but from that of the woman herself.

Rescued by a Coquette is generally considered one of the best Yuan Dynasty comedies. The battle of wits between the singsong girl Paner and Zhou. She helps us to understand the hypocrisy and cruelty of the privileged elite—Zhou is an official's son—and the unselfish affection and fair-mindedness of the ordinary man and woman, which enabled Paner and her friend to triumph in the end.

The dialogue in Act III, when Zhou She meets Paner and again when she urges him to write a divorce paper for Yinzhang, reveals his craftiness and her wit and courage. It is worth noting that the tactics Paner uses against Zhou She are the same which he and other profligates employ to cheat singsong girls. The girls have so often been deceived that they are on the alert and know how to turn the tables—a logical development.

Just as the playwright probes deep into Zhou She's character, he gives no superficial description of Paner but reveals her real self by presenting her innermost thoughts as the action develops. When Yinzhang's mother shows Paner her daughter's letter and asks for her help, Paner's first impulse is to refuse because her advice was ignored when Yinzhang married Zhou She. But then the thought of the hardships of all singsong girls and the bonds between them finally decides her to go, disclosing her fine character. On the way to rescue her friend, it occurs to her that she may meet women of good family; and comparing her own behaviour and social status with theirs, she despairs of ever being able to overcome the faults she has picked up in her trade. In this soliloquy she pours out the bitterness of the singsong girls so despised in feudal society.

Death of the Winged-Tiger General is a historical play about events which took place at the beginning of the tenth century. The hero, Li Cunxiao, has won many battles for Li Keyong, the Tartar prince. But two wicked men, Li Cunxin and Kang Junli, who please the prince by their skill in singing and dancing, slander the hero and have him torn to pieces. This reflects the corruption of feudal ruling circles.

This Tartar prince, Li Keyong, won favour by helping the Tang government to crush the peasant revolt led by Huang Chao at the end of the Tang Dynasty. Li Cunxiao was one of his ablest generals and his adopted son. The author, whose understanding was limited by historical conditions, could not see the reactionary nature of a general who suppressed a peasant revolt, and considered him instead as a hero, a positive character. It is worth noting that the general's tragic end was due not only to slander but to the fact that he was not Li Keyong's own son. In the Yuan Dynasty there was sharp rivalry between different nationalities, and Guan Hanqing in this play clearly implies that those who serve the invaders will come to a bad end. The two villains here are trusted by the prince only because they know the Tartar language and flatter their master. The appearance of such characters on the stage must undoubtedly have reminded contemporary audiences of those who collaborated with the conquerors.

Lord Guan Goes to the Feast is a historical drama that has remained popular for the last seven hundred years. According to tradition, Liu Bei, the king of Shu in the Three Kingdoms Period, was a good monarch who loved the people, while his rival Cao Cao of the Kingdom of Wei was a crafty and cruel ruler. Lord Guan defended Liu Bei's territory against Cao Cao and Sun Quan of the Kingdom of Wu. We need not concern ourselves here with the real character of these three rivals, but Lord Guan was a popular hero in the Yuan Dynasty on account of his loyalty to Liu Bei. Guan Hanqing was able most effectively to bring this heroic figure to life on the stage.

The Confucian concept of an "orthodox government" was an ideological weapon used by the feudal rulers to control the country, but during a period of foreign domination the people could turn this concept to account as a unifying factor against aggression. Thus this play had a positive significance for that period because through the hero's speeches Guan Hanqing upheld the ideal of Han orthodoxy.

Guan Hanqing stands out in the history of Chinese drama for his strong fighting spirit. He could not tolerate the social injustice of his time, and exposed it so forcefully that his audiences could see the cause of their suffering and knew what to attack in real life. Indeed, his plays are filled with heroic characters whose struggles and victories inspired the people to fight against abuses in society. Moreover his intricate, well-constructed plots show clearly how his heroes and heroines expose their enemies and unite with their friends, and what stratagems they use to defeat their opponents. He teaches that those who uphold justice, provided they plan well and use the right tactics, can defeat any foe no matter how powerful. Tan Jier, Paner and Lord Guan have formidable enemies; but because their cause is right and their tactics correct, they triumph in the end.

Guan Hanqing's technical brilliance is also outstanding. The climaxes of his plays nearly always grow out of the environment and the special characteristics of his heroes and heroines, who are magnificently alive thanks to the inspired detail with which he draws them, revealing their mental conflicts. He shows great psychological insight in his treatment of his heroes and heroines during a crisis. For example, before Paner goes to Zhengzhou she tells Yinzhang's mother of her sympathy for her friend; when Dou E takes a final leave of her mother-in-law, she is firm to the end because she has lived up to her principles all her life; Lord Guan's advice to his sons before setting out to the feast shows his concern for the younger generation. Similar episodes, moving and authentic, can be found in all these plays.

Guan Hanqing also shows a sure touch when he uses certain episodes to throw his characters into strong relief or build up atmosphere. For instance, at the end of Act I in *The Wife-Snatcher,* Zhang Gui picks up the pellet with which Lu Zhai-lang has hit his child, and bows to it saying:

This shot served as a go-between,
Coming like a bolt from the blue.

You will have a wife tomorrow,
But I shall have none.

This expresses the agony which Zhang cannot disclose to his wife, and at the same time suggests to the audience that in the next scene husband and wife will be parted. Again, in Act III of *The Riverside Pavilion,* when Tan Jier comes up with a fish and describes how she has caught it with her net, the audience foresees that she will spread a net to catch Lord Yang too. In Act IV of *Lord Guan Goes to the Feast,* the songs which Lord Guan sings when arriving and leaving about the magnificent scenery of the Changjiang (Yangtze) and the gallantry of the brave men who have fought there are powerfully evocative.

Guan Hanqing depicts positive characters by the use of meticulous detail, while his villains are usually caricatures, their ugliest features sketched in with simple strokes. This difference in treatment was partly due to the fact that Yuan Dynasty dramatists generally placed the main emphasis on the chief character who did all the singing, but it also shows where Guan Hanqing's sympathy lay. Feeling a genuine antipathy for the bullies and hypocrites, he could lay his finger on their essential weakness, expose them and make them ridiculous to his audiences.

As a keen observer of life, Guan Hanqing was able to present various social phenomena on the stage and raise new problems. Since all his plots are taken from real life, they remain fresh and convincing.

To appreciate Guan Hanqing's greatness, we. must remember that he lived seven hundred years ago in a feudal society during an age of sharp class and racial conflicts. The stage conventions of that time were most exacting, as indicated earlier. The number of acts was strictly limited, and there could only be one chief character, while the tunes and songs were also governed by inflexible rules. The songs in each act must belong to the same musical scale and follow a definite pattern. The requirements of the music determined the length of the lines as well as the words accented. In those days, the songs or lyrical part of the drama were all important, while the dialogue was merely secondary. This tradition persisted till the fourteenth century, and it was only after a new form of drama, the Ming Dynasty *zhuan-qi,* became popular that there was a gradual introduction of more dialogue.

Guan Hanqing's plays exemplify the best qualities of many dramatists of his time. He helped to found the realist tradition in the classical Chinese theatre, and have had a deep and lasting influence. But since his plays exposed various abuses in feudal society and offended the privileged classes, from the fourteenth century onwards they were not highly regarded by the literati. This is why many of them have been lost. Today when the people are masters of their own fate, this great dramatist who had such faith in the common man is coming back into his own, a new edition of his works has been published, and his plays are being staged again.

Though the dates of Guan Hanqing's birth and death are uncertain, we know that seven centuries ago he was writing for the stage, and this year has therefore been chosen as his 700th anniversary. We are publishing these English translations of some of his plays in order to introduce this great thirteenth century playwright to lovers of the drama throughout the world.

March 1958

SNOW IN MIDSUMMER

CHARACTERS
MISTRESS CAI, *a widow*
DOU TIANZHANG, *a poor scholar, later a government inspector*
DOU E, *Dou Tianzhang's daughter Duanyun*
DOCTOR LU
OLD ZHANG DONKEY, *his son*
PREFECT
ATTENDANT
THE OFFICER IN CHARGE OF EXECUTIONS
EXECUTIONER

ACT I

(Enter Mistress Cai.)

MRS. CAI:

A flower may blossom again,
But youth never returns.

I am Mistress Cai of Chuzhou. There were three of us in my family; but unluckily my husband died, leaving me just one son who is eight years old. We live together, mother and son, and are quite well off. A scholar named Dou of Shan-yang Prefecture borrowed five taels of silver from me last year. Now the interest and capital come to ten taels, and I've asked several times for the money; but Mr. Dou cannot pay it. He has a daughter, and I've a good mind to make her my daughter-in-law; then he won't have to pay back the ten taels. Mr. Dou chose today as a lucky day, and is bringing the girl to me; so I won't ask him to pay me back, but wait for him at home. He should be here soon. *(Enter Dou Tianzhang, leading his daughter Duanyun.)*

DOU:

I am master of all the learning in the world,
But my fate is worse than that of other men.

My name is Dou Tianzhang, and the home of my ancestors is Chang-an. I have studied the classics since I was a child and read a good deal; but I haven't yet taken the examinations. Unfortunately my wife has died, leaving me this only daughter, Duanyun. She lost her mother when she was three, and now she is seven. Living from hand to mouth, I moved to Shanyang Prefecture in Chuzhou and took lodgings here. There is a widow in this town named Cai, who lives alone with her son and is fairly well off, and as I had no money for travelling I borrowed five taels from her. Now, with the interest, I owe her ten taels; but though she has asked several times for the money, I haven't been able to pay her. And recently she has sent to say she would like my daughter to marry her son. Since the spring examinations will soon be starting, I should be going to the capital; but I have no money for the road. So I am forced to take Duanyun to Widow Cai as her future daughter-in-law. I'm not marrying my daughter but selling her! For this means the widow will cancel my debt and give me some cash for my journey. This is all I can hope for. Ah, child, your father does this against his will! While talking to myself I've reached her door. Mistress Cai! Are you at home? *(Enter Mistress Cai.)*

MRS. CAI:

So it's Mr. Dou! Come in, please. I've been waiting for you. *(They greet each other.)*

DOU:

I've brought you my daughter, ma'am, not to be your daughter-in-law—that would be asking too much—but to serve you day and night. I must be going to take the examination. I hope you will look after her.

MRS. CAI:

Well, you owed me ten taels including interest. Here is your promissory note back and another two taels for your journey. I hope you don't think it too little.

DOU:

Thank you, ma'am! Instead of asking for what I owe you, you have given me money for the road. Some day I shall repay your kindness in full. My daughter is a foolish child. Please take care of her, ma'am, for my sake.

MRS. CAI:

Don't worry, Mr. Dou. I shall look after your daughter as if she were my own.

DOU

(kneeling to her): If the child deserves a beating, ma'am, for my sake just scold her! And if she deserves a scolding, for my sake speak gently to her! As for you, Duanyun, this isn't like at home, where your father used to put up with your whims. If you're naughty here, you'll be beaten and cursed. When shall I see you again, child? *(He sighs.)*

I drum sadly on my sheath;
I have studied the Confucian classics;
My unhappy wife died young,
And now I am parted from my only daughter. (Exit.)

MRS. CAI:

Now Mr. Dou has left me his daughter, and gone to the capital for the examination. I must see to the house. *(Exeunt.)*
(Enter Doctor Lu.)

DOCTOR:

I diagnose all diseases with care,
And prescribe as the Herbal dictates;
But I cannot bring dead men back to life,
And the live ones I treat often die.

I am Doctor Lu. I own a drug shop here. I've borrowed ten taels of silver from Mistress Cai of this town, and with interest now owe her twenty taels. She keeps coming for the money; but I haven't got it. If she doesn't come back, so much the better. If she does, I have a plan. I'll sit in my shop now, and wait to see who turns up. *(Enter Mistress Cai.)*

MRS. CAI:

I am Mistress Cai. Thirteen years ago Mr. Dou Tianzhang left his daughter Duanyun with me to marry my son, and I changed her name to Dou E. But after their marriage my son died, so now she's a widow. That was nearly three years ago, and she'll soon be out of mourning. I've told her that I'm going to town to collect a debt from Doctor Lu. Now I've reached his house. Is Doctor Lu in?

DOCTOR:

Yes, ma'am, come in.

MRS. CAI:

You've kept my money for a long time, doctor. You must pay me back.

DOCTOR:

I've no money at home, ma'am. If you'll come with me to the village, I'll get money for you.

MRS. CAI:

Very well. I'll go with you. *(They start walking.)*

DOCTOR:

Now we are outside the city. Here's a good spot, with no one about. Why not do it here? I've got the rope ready. Who's that calling you, ma'am?

MRS. CAI:

Where?

(The Doctor strangles the widow with the rope. Enter Old Zhang and his son Donkey. As they rush forward the Doctor takes to his heels. Old Zhang revives Mistress Cai.)

DONKEY:

It's an old woman, dad, nearly strangled to death.

ZHANG:

Hey, you! Who are you? What's your name? Why did that fellow try to strangle you?

MRS. CAI:

My name is Cai and I live in town with my widowed daughter-in-law. Doctor Lu owes me twenty taels so he lured me here and tried to strangle me. If not for you and this young man, it would have been all up with me!

DONKEY:

Did you hear that, dad? She has a daughter-in-law at home! Suppose you take her as your wife and I take the daughter-in-law? Propose it to her, dad!

ZHANG:

Hey, widow! You've no husband and I've no wife. How about the two of us getting married?

MRS. CAI:

What an idea! I shall give you a handsome sum of money to thank you.

DONKEY:

So you refuse! I'd better strangle you after all.

MRS. CAI:

Wait! Let me think a moment, brother!

DONKEY:

What do you need to think for? You take my dad, and I'll take your daughter-in-law.

MRS. CAI *(aside)*:

If I don't agree he'll strangle me! *(To them.)* Very well. Come home with me, both of you.

DONKEY:

Let's go. *(Exeunt.) (Enter Dou E.)*

DOU E:

I am Duanyun, and my home was in Chuzhou. When I was three I lost my mother; and when I was seven I had to leave my father, for he sent me to Mistress Cai as her son's child-bride, and she changed my name to Dou E. At seventeen I married; but unluckily my husband died three years ago. Now I am twenty. There is a Doctor Lu in town who owes my mother-in-law twenty taels including interest; and though she has asked him several times for the money, he hasn't paid her back. She's gone today to try to collect the debt. Ah, when shall I escape from my misery?

My heart is full of grief,
I have suffered for so many years!
Morning or evening it is all the same:
From dawn to dusk I can neither eat nor sleep,
Racked by sad dreams at night, sad thoughts by day,
Unending sorrow which I cannot banish,
Unceasing reasons for fresh misery.

Wretchedness makes me weep, grief makes me frown;
Will this never come to an end?
Is it my fate to be wretched all my life?
Who else knows grief like mine?
For my sorrow, like flowing water, never ceases.
At three I lost my mother, at seven was torn from my father;
Then the life of the husband I married was cut short;
So my mother-in-law and I are left as widows,
With no one to care for us or see to our needs.
Did I burn too little incense in my last life
That my marriage was unlucky?
We should all do good betimes;
So I mourn for my husband and serve my mother-in-law,
Obedient to all her bidding.

My mother-in-law has been gone a long time to collect that debt. What can be keeping her?

(Enter Mistress Cai with Old Zhang and Donkey.)

MRS. CAI:

Wait here at the door while I go in.

DONKEY:

All right, mother. Go in and tell her her husband is at the door. *(Mistress Cai sees Dou E.)*

DOU E:

So you're back, mother. Have you had a meal?

MRS. CAI *(crying)*:

Ah, poor child! How am I going to break this to you?

DOU E:

I see her in floods of tears,
Hiding some grief in her heart;
Greeting her quickly,
I beg her to tell me the reason.

MRS. CAI:

How can I say this?

24

DOU E:

> *She's shilly-shallying and looks ashamed.*
> What has upset you, mother? Why are you crying?

MRS. CAI:

> When I asked Doctor Lu for the silver, he lured me outside the town, then tried to strangle me; but an old man called Zhang and his son Donkey saved my life. Now Old Zhang is going to marry me: that's why I'm upset.

DOU E:

> That would never do, mother! Please think again! We're not short of money. Besides, you are growing old—how can you take another husband?

MRS. CAI:

> Child, I couldn't do anything else!

DOU E:

> Mother, listen to me!
> *What will become of you*
> *If you choose a day and solemnize a wedding?*
> *Now your hair is as white as snow,*
> *How can you wear the bright silk veil of a bride?*
> *No wonder they say it is hard to keep women at home,*
> *If at sixty, when all thought of love should be over,*
> *You've forgotten your former husband,*
> *And taken a fancy to another man!*
> *This will make others split their sides with laughter!*
> *Yes, split their sides with laughter!*
> *Like the widow who fanned her husband's tomb,*
> *You're no tender bamboo shoot, no tender shoot.*
> *How can you paint your eyebrows and remarry?*
> *Your husband left you his property,*
> *Made provision for the future,*
> *For daily food and a good livelihood,*
> *So that you and your son could remain beholden to no one,*
> *And live to a ripe old age.*

Did he go to such trouble for nothing?

MRS. CAI:

Since it has come to this, I think you'd better take a husband too, and today can be the wedding day.

DOU E:

You take a husband if you must. I won't!

MRS. CAI:

The date is fixed, and they are already here.

DONKEY:

Now we shall marry into their family. Our hats are brushed as good as new, and have narrow brims like bridegrooms'! Good! Fine!

DOU E:

Stand back, you fellows!
Women should not believe all men say;
Such a marriage could not last.
Where did she find this old yokel,
And this other ruffian here?
Have you no feeling left for the dead?
You must think this over again.
Your husband worked in different cities and counties
To amass a well-earned fortune, and lack nothing.
How can you let his estate go to Donkey Zhang?
He tilled the land, but others are reaping the harvest.

(Exit.)

ZHANG *(to Mrs. Cai):*

Let us go and drink, ma'am.
(Exeunt.)

DONKEY:

Dou E refuses to have me, but I shan't let her get away: she will have to be my wife. Now I'll drink with my old man! *(Exit.)*

26

ACT II

(Enter Doctor Lu.)

DOCTOR:

I am Doctor Lu. I lured Mistress Cai outside the town and was just going to strangle her when two men rescued her. Today I am opening shop. I wonder who will turn up.

(Enter Donkey)

DONKEY:

I am Donkey Zhang. Dou E still refuses to marry me. Now the old woman is ill, I'm going to poison her; for once the old one is dead, the young one will have to be my wife. Ah, here is a drug shop. Doctor! I want a drug!

DOCTOR:

What drug do you want?

DONKEY:

I want some poison.

DOCTOR:

Who dares sell you poison? How can you ask such a thing?

DONKEY:

You won't let me have it then?

DOCTOR:

I won't. What are you going to do about it?

DONKEY *(seizing him):*

Fine! Fine! Aren't you the man who tried to murder Mistress Cai? Do you think I don't recognize you? I'll take you to court.

DOCTOR *(in panic):*

Let me go, brother! I've got it! I've got it! *(Gives him the poison.)*

DONKEY:

> Now that I've got the poison, I'm going home.
> *(Exit)*

DOCTOR:

> So that man who came to buy poison was one of the men who rescued the widow. Since I've given him poison, he may get me into further trouble later. I'd better close my shop and go to Zhuozhou to sell drugs. *(Exit.)*
>
> *(Enter Mistress Cai, supported by Old Zhang and Donkey.)*

ZHANG:

> I came to Mistress Cai's house hoping to be her second husband. Who would have thought that the widow would fall ill? I am really too unlucky. If there's anything you fancy to eat, ma'am, just let me know.

MRS. CAI:

> I'd like some mutton tripe soup.

ZHANG:

> Son, go and tell Dou E to make some mutton tripe soup for her mother-in-law.

DONKEY:

> Dou E! Your mother-in-law wants some mutton tripe soup. Look sharp about it! *(Enter Dou E.)*

DOU E:

> I am Dou E. My mother-in-law is unwell and wants some mutton tripe soup, so I've made her some. When you think of it, some women are too fickle!
>
> *She wants to lie with a husband all her life,*
> *Unwilling to sleep alone;*
> *First she married one, and now she has picked another.*
> *Some women never speak of household matters,*
> *But pick up all the gossip,*
> *Describe their husbands' adventures,*

And are always up to some low tricks themselves.
Is there one like Lady Zhuo,[2] who stooped to serve in a tavern?
Or like Meng Guang,[3] who showed such respect to her husband?
The women today are different:
You can neither tell their character from their speech,
Nor judge them by their actions.
They're all of them faithless, all run after new lovers;
And before their husbands' graves are dry
They set aside their mourning for new clothes.
Where is the woman whose tears for her husband
Caused the Great Wall to crumble?[4]
Where is she who left her washing
And drowned herself in the stream?[5]
Where is she who changed into stone
Through longing for her husband?[6]
How shameful that women today are so unfaithful,
So few of them are chaste, so many wanton!
All, all are gone, those virtuous women of old;
For wives will not cleave to their husbands!

---

[2] Zhuo Wenjun, the daughter of a rich man, who eloped with Sima Xiangru, a famous Han Dynasty scholar. Since they were poor, they kept a small tavern in Chengdu where she served as barmaid.

[3] Wife of Liang Hong of the Later Han Dynasty.

[4] Thousands of the men conscripted by the First Emperor of Qin to build the Great Wall died. According to a legend Meng Jiangnu, the wife of one of these conscripts, wept so bitterly at the wall that part of it crumbled.

[5] During the Spring and Autumn Period (770-475 B.C.), Wu Zixu fled from the state of Chu to Wu. A woman washing by a river took pity on him and fed him. Upon leaving, he asked her not to tell his pursuers which way he had gone. To set his mind at rest she drowned herself.

[6] This legendary woman, whose husband left home, climbed a hill every day to watch for his return, till at last she was transformed into a boulder.

Now the soup is ready. I had better take it in.

DONKEY:

Let me take it to her. *(He takes the bowl.)* This hasn't much flavour. Bring some salt and vinegar. *(Dou E goes out. Donkey puts poison in the soup. Dou E comes back.)*

DOU E:

Here are the salt and vinegar.

DONKEY:

Put some in.

DOU E:

You say that it lacks salt and vinegar,
Adding these will improve the flavour.
I hope my mother will be better soon,
And the soup will serve as a cordial.
Then the three of you can live happily together.

ZHANG:

Son, is the soup ready?

DONKEY:

Here it is. Take it.

ZHANG *(taking the soup):*

Have some soup, ma'am.

MRS. CAI:

I am sorry to give you so much trouble. You have some first.

ZHANG:

Won't you try it?

MRS. CAI:

No, I want *you* to drink it first.
(Old Zhang drinks the soup.)

DOU E:

One says: "Won't you try it?"
The other says: "You have it!"
What a shameful way to talk!
How can I help being angry?
The new couple is in transports;
Forgetting her first husband,
She listens to this new man's lightest word.
Now her heart is like a willow seed in the breeze,
Not steadfast as a rock.
Old love is nothing to new love:
She wants to live with this new man for ever,
Without a thought for the other man far away.

ZHANG:

Why has this soup made me dizzy? *(He falls to the ground.)*

MRS. CAI:

Why should you feel unwell after that soup? *(Panic-stricken.)* Take a grip on yourself, old man! Don't give up so easily! *(Wails.)*

DOU E:

It's no use grieving for him;
All mortal men must die when their time is up.
Some fall ill, some meet with accidents;
Some catch a chill, some are struck down by heat;
Some die of hunger, surfeit or over-work;
But every death has its cause,
Human life is ruled by fate,
And no man can control it,
For our span of life is predestined.
He has been here a few days only;
He is not of your family,
And he never sent you wedding gifts:
Sheep, wine, silk or money.

For a time you stayed together,
But now he is dead and gone!
I am not an unfilial daughter,
But I fear what the neighbours may say;
So stop your moaning and wailing:
He is not the man you married as a girl. (Old Zhang dies.)

MRS. CAI:

What shall we do? He's dead!

DOU E:

He's no relation—I have no tears for him.
There's no need to be so overcome with grief,
Or to cry so bitterly and lose your head!

DONKEY:

Fine! You've poisoned my father! What are you going to do about it?

MRS. CAI:

Child, you had better marry him now.

DOU E:

How can you say such a thing, mother?
This fellow forced my mother-in-law to keep him;
Now he's poisoned his father,
But whom does he think he can frighten?

MRS. CAI:

You'd better marry him, child.

DOU E:

A horse can't have two saddles;
I was your son's wife when he was alive,
Yet now you are urging me to marry again.
This is unthinkable!

DONKEY:

Dou E, you murdered my old man. Do you want to settle this in private or settle it in public?

DOU E:

What do you mean?

DONKEY:

If you want it settled in public, I'll drag you to the court, and you'll have to confess to the murder of my father! If you want it settled in private, agree to be my wife. Then I'll let you off.

DOU E:

I am innocent. I'll go with you to the prefect. *(Donkey drags Dou E and Mistress Cai out.)*

ACT III

(Enter the Prefect with an Attendant)

PREFECT:

I am a hard-working official;
I make money out of my lawsuits;
But when my superiors come to investigate,
I pretend to be ill and stay at home in bed.

I am prefect of Chuzhou. This morning I am holding court. Attendant, summon the court! *(The Attendant gives a shout.)*

(Enter Donkey, dragging in Dou E and Mistress Cai.)

DONKEY:

I want to lodge a charge.

ATTENDANT:

Come over here.
(Donkey and Dou E kneel to the Prefect, who kneels to them!)

PREFECT *(kneeling):*

Please rise.

ATTENDANT:

Your Honour, this is a citizen who's come to ask for justice. Why should you kneel to him?

PREFECT:

Why? Because such citizens are food and clothes to me!
(The Attendant assents.)

PREFECT:

Which of you is the plaintiff, which the defendant? Out with the truth now!

DONKEY:

I am the plaintiff. I accuse this young woman, Dou E, of poisoning my father with soup. Let justice be done, Your Honour!

PREFECT:

Who poisoned the soup?

DOU E:

Not I!

MRS. CAI:

Not I!

DONKEY:

Not I!

PREFECT:

If none of you did it, I wonder if I could have done it?

DOU E:

Your Honour is as discerning as a mirror,
And can see my innermost thoughts.
There was nothing wrong with the soup,
I know nothing about the poison;
He made a pretence of tasting it,
Then his father drank it and fell down dead.
It is not that I want to deny my guilt in court;
But I cannot confess to a crime I have not committed!

PREFECT:

Low characters are like that: they'll only confess when put to torture. Attendant! Bring the bastinado to beat her.
(The Attendant beats Dou E. Three times she faints and he has to sprinkle her with water to bring her round.)

DOU E:

This terrible beating is more than I can bear.
You brought this on yourself, mother. Why complain?
May all women in the world who marry again
Be warned by me!
Why are they shouting so fiercely?
I groan with pain;

I come to myself, then faint away again.
A thousand strokes: I am streaming with blood!
At each blow from the bastinado
My blood spurts out and my skin is torn from my flesh;
My spirit takes flight in fear,
Approaching the nether regions.
Who knows the bitterness in my heart?
It was not I who poisoned the old man;
I beg Your Honour to find out the truth!

PREFECT:

Will you confess now?

DOU E:

I swear it was not I who put in the poison.

PREFECT:

In that case, beat the old woman.

DOU E *(hastily)*:

Stop, stop! Don't beat my mother-in-law! Rather than that, I'll say I poisoned the old man.

PREFECT:

Fasten her in the cangue and throw her into the gaol for the condemned. Tomorrow she shall be taken to the market-place to be executed.

MRS. CAI *(weeping)*:

Dou E, my child! It's because of me you are losing your life. Oh, this will be the death of me!

DOU E:

When I am a headless ghost, unjustly killed,
Do you think I will spare that scoundrel?
Men cannot be deceived for ever,
And Heaven will see this injustice.
I struggled as hard as I could, but now I am helpless;
I was forced to confess that I poisoned the old man;

37

> *How could I let you be beaten, mother?*
> *How could I save you except by dying myself?*
> *(She is led off)*

DONKEY:

If she's to be killed tomorrow, I'll hang around. *(Exit.)*

MRS. CAI:

Poor child! Tomorrow she will be killed in the marketplace. This will be the death of me! *(Exit.)*

PREFECT:

Tomorrow Dou E will be executed. Today's work is done. Bring me my horse; I am going home to drink. *(Exeunt.)*

(Enter the Officer in charge)

OFFICER:

I am the officer in charge of executions. Today we are putting a criminal to death. We must stand guard at the end of the road, to see that no one comes through.

(Enter the Attendants. They beat the drum and the gong three times; then the executioner enters, sharpens his sword and waves a flag. Dou E is led on in a cangue. The gong and drum are beaten)

EXECUTIONER:

Get a move on! Let no one pass this way.

DOU E:

> *Through no fault of mine I am called a criminal,*
> *And condemned to be beheaded—*
> *I cry out to Heaven and Earth of this injustice!*
> *I reproach both Earth and Heaven*
> *For they would not save me.*
> *The sun and moon give light by day and by night,*
> *Mountains and rivers watch over the world of men;*
> *Yet Heaven cannot tell the innocent from the guilty;*
> *And confuses the wicked with the good!*

The good are poor, and die before their time;
The wicked are rich, and live to a great old age.
The gods are afraid of the mighty and bully the weak;
They let evil take its course.
Ah, Earth! you will not distinguish good from bad,
And, Heaven! you let me suffer this injustice!
Tears pour down my cheeks in vain!

EXECUTIONER:

Get a move on! We are late.

DOU E:

The cangue round my neck makes me stagger this way and that,
And I'm jostled backward and forward by the crowd.
Will you do me a favour, brother?

EXECUTIONER:

What do you want?

DOU E:

If you take me the front way, I shall bear you a grudge;
If you take me the back way, I shall die content.
Please do not think me wilful!

EXECUTIONER:

Now that you're going to the execution ground, are there any relatives you want to see?

DOU E:

I am going to die. What relatives do I need?

EXECUTIONER:

Why did you ask me just now to take you the back way?

DOU E:

Please don't go by the front street, brother,
But take me by the back street.
The other way my mother-in-law might see me.

EXECUTIONER:

You can't escape death, so why worry if she sees you?

DOU E:

If my mother-in-law were to see me in chains being led to the execution ground—
She would burst with indignation!
She would burst with indignation!
Please grant me this comfort, brother, before I die!
(Enter Mistress Cai.)

MRS. CAI:

Ah, Heaven! Isn't that my daughter-in-law? This will be the death of me!

EXECUTIONER:

Stand back, old woman!

DOU E:

Let her come closer so that I can say a few words to her.

EXECUTIONER:

Hey, old woman! Come here. Your daughter-in-law wants to speak to you.

MRS. CAI:

Poor child! This will be the death of me!

DOU E:

Mother, when you were unwell and asked for mutton tripe soup, I prepared some for you. Donkey Zhang made me fetch more salt and vinegar so that he could poison the soup, and then told me to give it to you. He didn't know his old man would drink it. Donkey Zhang poisoned the soup to kill you, so that he could force me to be his wife. He never thought his father would die instead. To take revenge, he dragged me to court. Because I didn't want you to suffer, I had to confess to murder, and now I am going to be killed. In future, mother, if you have gruel to spare, give me half a bowl; and if you have paper money to spare, burn some for me, for the sake of your dead son!

> *Take pity on one who is dying an unjust death;*
> *Take pity on one whose head will be struck from her body;*
> *Take pity on one who has worked with you in your home;*
> *Take pity on one who has neither mother nor father;*
> *Take pity on one who has served you all these years;*
> *And at festivals offer my spirit a bowl of cold gruel.*

MRS. CAI *(weeping):*

Don't worry. Ah, this will be the death of me!

DOU E:

> *Burn some paper coins to my headless corpse,*
> *For the sake of your dead son.*
> *We wail and complain to Heaven:*
> *There is no justice! Dou E is wrongly slain!*

EXECUTIONER:

Now then, old woman, stand back! The time has come.

(Dou E kneels, and the Executioner removes the cangue from her neck!)

DOU E:

I want to say three things, officer. If you will let me, I shall die content. I want a clean mat and a white silk streamer twelve feet long to hang on the flag-pole. When the sword strikes off my head, not a drop of my warm blood will stain the ground. It will all fly up instead to the white silk streamer. This is the hottest time of summer, sir. If injustice has indeed been done, three feet of snow will cover my dead body. Then this district will suffer from drought for three whole years.

EXECUTIONER:

Be quiet! What a thing to say! *(The Executioner waves his flag.)*

DOU E:

> *A dumb woman was blamed for poisoning herself;*

A buffalo is whipped while it toils for its master.

EXECUTIONER:

Why is it suddenly so overcast? It is snowing! *(He prays to Heaven!)*

DOU E:

Once Zou Yan caused frost to appear:[7]
Now snow will show the injustice done to me!
(The Executioner beheads her, and the Attendant sees to her body!)

EXECUTIONER:

A fine stroke! Now let us go and have a drink. *(The Attendants assent, and carry the body off.)*

---

[7] Zou Yan of the Warring States Period (475-221 B.C.) was a loyal subject of the Prince of Yan, but because an enemy slandered him he was imprisoned. Since such great injustice had been done, frost appeared in summer.

ACT IV

(Enter Dou Tianzhang)

DOU:

I am Dou Tianzhang. It is thirteen years since I left my child Duanyun. I went to the capital, passed the examination and was made a counsellor. And because I am able, just and upright, the emperor appointed me Inspector of the Huai River Area. I have travelled from place to place investigating cases, and I have the sword of authority and golden tally so that I can punish corrupt officials without first reporting to the throne. My heart is torn between grief and happiness. I am glad because I am a high official responsible for seeing that justice is done. I am sad, though, because when Duanyun was seven I gave her to Mistress Cai; and after I became an official and sent for news of the widow to Chuzhou, the neighbours said she had moved away—to what place they did not know—and there has been no word since. I have wept for my child till my eyes are dim and my hair is white. Now I have come south of the Huai River, and am wondering why this district has had no rain for three years. I shall rest in the district office, boy. Tell the local officers they need not call today. I shall see them early tomorrow.

感天動地竇娥冤

SERVANT *(calling out):*

The officers and secretaries are not to call on His Excellency today. He will see them early tomorrow.

DOU:

Tell the secretaries of the different departments to send all their cases here for my inspection. I shall study some under the lamp.

(The Servant brings him the files)

DOU:

Light the lamp for me. You have been working hard, and you may rest now. But come when I call you.

(The Servant lights the lamp and leaves)

DOU:

I shall go through a few cases. Here is one concerning Dou E, who poisoned her father-in-law. Curious that the first culprit's surname should be the same as mine! To murder one's father-in-law is one of the unpardonable crimes; so it seems there are lawless elements among my clan. Since this case has been dealt with, I need not read it. I'll put it at the bottom of the pile and look at another. Wait, I suddenly feel drowsy. I suppose I am growing old, and am tired after travelling. I will take a short nap on the desk. *(He sleeps)*

(Enter Dou E's ghost)

DOU E:

Day after day I weep in the underworld,
Waiting impatiently for my revenge.
I pace on slowly in darkness,
Then am borne along by the whirlwind;
Enveloped by mist I come swiftly in ghostly form.

(She looks about her.) Now the door-gods will not let me pass. I am the daughter of Inspector Dou. Though I died unjustly, my father does not know it; so I have come to visit him in his dreams. *(She enters the room and weeps)*

DOU *(shedding tears):*

Duanyun, my child! Where have you been? *(Dou E's spirit leaves, and Dou wakes up)*

How odd! I fell asleep and dreamed that I saw my daughter coming towards me; but where is she now? Let me go on with these cases.

(Dou E's spirit enters and makes the lamp burn low.) Strange! I was just going to read a case when the light flickered and dimmed. My servant is asleep; I must trim the wick myself. *(As he trims the lamp, Dou E's spirit rearranges the file.)* Now the light is brighter, I can read again. "This concerns the criminal Dou E, who poisoned her father-in-law." Strange! I read this case first, and put it under the others. How has it come to the top? Since this case has already been dealt with, let me put it at the bottom again and study a different one. *(Once more Dou E's spirit makes the lamp burn low.)* Strange! Why is the light flickering again? I must trim it once more. *(As Dou trims the light, Dou E's spirit once more turns over the file)* Now the lamp is brighter, I can read another case. "This concerns the criminal Dou E, who poisoned her father-in-law." How extraordinary! I definitely put this at the bottom of the pile just before I trimmed the lamp. How has it come to the top again? Can there be ghosts in this office? Well, ghost or no ghost, an injustice must have been done. Let me put this underneath and read another. *(Dou E's spirit makes the lamp burn low again.)* Strange! The lamp is flickering again. Can there actually be a ghost here tampering with it? I'll trim it once more. *(As he trims the wick, Dou E's spirit comes up to him and he sees her. He strikes his sword on the desk)* Ah, there's the ghost! I warn you, I am the emperor's inspector of justice. If you come near, I'll cut you in two. Hey, boy! How can you sleep so soundly? Get up at once! Ghosts! Ghosts! This is terrifying!

DOU E:

Fear is making him lose his head;
The sound of my weeping has frightened him more than ever.

Here, Dou Tianzhang, my old father,

> *Will you let your daughter Dou E bow to you?*

DOU:

You say I am your father, ghost, and offer to bow to me as my daughter. Aren't you mistaken? My daughter's name is Duanyun. When she was seven she was given to Mistress Cai as a child-bride. You call yourself by a different name, Dou E. How can you be my child?

DOU E:

After you gave me to Mistress Cai, father, she changed my name to Dou E.

DOU:

So you say you are my child Duanyun. Let me ask you this: Are you the woman accused of murdering her father-in-law and executed?

DOU E:

I am.

DOU:

Hush, girl! I've wept for you till my eyes grew dim, and worried for you till my hair turned white. How did you come to be condemned for this most heinous of crimes? I am a high official now, whose duty it is to see that justice is done. I have come here to investigate cases and discover corrupt officials. You are my child, but you are guilty of the worst crime of all. If I could not control you, how can I control others? When I married you to the widow's son, I expected you to observe the Three Duties and Four Virtues. The Three Duties are obedience to your father before marriage, obedience to your husband after marriage, and obedience to your son after your husband's death. The Four Virtues are to serve your parents-in-law, to show respect to your husband, to remain on good terms with your sisters-in-law, and to live in peace with your neighbours. But regardless of your duties, you have committed the gravest crime of all! The proverb says: Look before you leap, or you may be sorry too late. For three generations no son of our clan has broken the law; for five generations no daughter has married again. As a married woman, you should have studied propriety and morality; but instead you perpetrated the most terrible crime. You have disgraced our ancestors and injured my good name. Tell me the whole truth at once, and nothing but the truth! If you utter one false word, I shall send you to the tutelary god; then your spirit will never re-enter human form, but remain a hungry ghost for ever in the shades.

DOU E:

Don't be so angry, father. Don't threaten me like an angry wolf or tiger! Let me explain this to you. At three, I lost my mother; at seven, I was parted from my father, when you sent me to Mistress Cai as her future daughter-in-law, and my name was changed to Dou E. At seventeen, I married; but unhappily two years later my husband died, and I stayed as a widow with my mother-in-law. In Chuzhou there lived a certain Doctor Lu, who owed my mother-in-law twenty taels of silver. One day when she went to ask him for the money, he lured her outside the town and tried to strangle her; but Donkey Zhang and his father came by and saved her life. Old Zhang asked: "Whom do you have in your family, ma'am?" My mother-in-law said: "No one but a widowed daughter-in-law." Old Zhang said: "In that case, I will marry you. What do you say?" When my mother-in-law refused, the two men said: "If you don't agree, we shall strangle you again!" So she was frightened into marrying him. Donkey tried to seduce me several times, but I always resisted him. One day my mother-in-law was unwell and wanted some mutton tripe soup. When I prepared it, Donkey told me to let him taste it. "It's good," he said. "But there's not enough salt and vinegar." When I went to fetch more, he secretly poisoned the soup and told me to take it to her. But my mother-in-law gave it to Old Zhang. Then blood spurted from the old man's mouth, nose, ears and eyes, and he died. At that Donkey said, "Dou E, you poisoned my father. Do you want to settle this in public or in private?" "What do you mean?" I asked. "If you want it settled in public," he said, "I shall take the case to court, and you will pay for my father's death with your life. If you want it settled in private, then be my wife." "A good horse won't have two saddles," I told him. "A good woman won't remarry. For three generations no son of our clan has broken the law; for five generations no daughter has married again. I'd rather die than be your wife. I am innocent. I'll go to court with you." Then he dragged me before the prefect. I was tried again and again, stripped and tortured; but I would rather have died than make a false confession. When the prefect saw that I wouldn't confess, he threatened to have my mother-in-law tortured; and because she was too old to stand the torture, I made a false confession. Then they took me to the execution ground to kill me. I made three vows before my death. First, I asked for a twelve-foot white silk streamer and swore that, if I was innocent, when the sword struck off my head no drop of my blood would stain the ground—it would all fly up to the streamer. Next I vowed that, though it was midsummer, Heaven would send down three feet of snow to cover my body. Last, I vowed that this district would suffer three years' drought. All these vows have come true, because of the crime against me.

> *I complained not to any official but to Heaven,*
> *For I could not express the injustice that was done me;*
> *And to save my mother from torture*
> *I confessed to a crime of which I was innocent,*
> *And remained true to my dead husband*
> *Three feet of snow fell on my corpse;*
> *My hot blood gushed to the white silk streamer;*
> *Zou Yan called down frost,*
> *And snow showed the injustice done me.*
> *Your child committed no crime,*
> *But suffered a great wrong:*
> *For resisting seduction I was executed!*
> *I would not disgrace my clan, so I lost my life!*
> *Day after day in the shades*
> *My spirit mourns alone.*
> *You are sent by the emperor with authority;*
> *Consider this case and this man's wickedness;*
> *Cut him in pieces and avenge my wrong!*

DOU *(weeping):*

Ah, my wrongly slain daughter, how this wrings my heart! Let me ask you this: Is it because of you that this district has suffered for three years from drought?

DOU E:

It is.

DOU:

So! This reminds me of a story. In the Han Dynasty there was a virtuous widow whose mother-in-law hanged herself, and whose sister-in-law accused her of murdering the old woman. The governor of Donge had her executed, but because of her unjust death there was no rain in. that district for three years. When Lord Yu came to investigate, he saw the dead woman's ghost carrying a plea and weeping before the hall; and after he changed the verdict, killed a bull and sacrificed at her grave there was a great downpour of rain. This case is rather similar to that. Tomorrow I shall right this wrong for you.

I bow my white head in sorrow
Over the innocent girl who was wrongly slain.
Now dawn is breaking, you had better leave me;
Tomorrow I shall set right this miscarriage of justice.

DOU E *(bowing):*

With sharp sword of authority and tally of gold, You will kill all evil and corrupt officials, To serve your sovereign and relieve the people! (She turns back) There's one thing I nearly forgot, father. My mother-in-law is old now, and has no one to look after her.

DOU:

This is dutiful, my child.

DOU E:

I ask my father to care for my mother-in-law,
For she is growing old. My father now
Will reopen my case and change the unjust verdict. (Exit.)

DOU:

Dawn is breaking. Call the local officers, and all those concerned in the case of Dou E.

SERVANT:

Yes, Your Excellency.

(The Prefect, Mistress Cai, Donkey Zhang and Doctor Lu are sent in. They kneel before Dou)

DOU:

Mistress Cai, do you recognize me?

MRS. CAI:

No, Your Excellency.

DOU:

I am Dou Tianzhang. Listen, all of you, to the verdict! Donkey Zhang murdered his father and blackmailed good citizens. He shall be executed in public. Let him be taken to the market-place to be killed. The prefect passed a wrong sentence. He shall be given one hundred strokes and have his name struck off the official list. Doctor Lu is guilty of selling poison. Let him be beheaded in the market-place. Mistress Cai shall be lodged in my house. The wrong sentence passed on Dou E shall be rescinded.

Let the Donkey be killed in public,
The prefect dismissed from office;
Then let us offer a great sacrifice
So that my daughter's spirit may go to heaven.
(THE END)

THE WIFE-SNATCHER

CHARACTERS
LU ZHAILANG, *a powerful bully*
ZHANG QIAN, *his servant*
LI SI, *a silversmith*
LI'S WIFE
HAPPY BOY, *Li's son*
SWEET MAID, *Li's daughter*
ZHANG GUI, *a clerk in the local government*
ZHANG'S WIFE
GOLDEN BOY, *Zhang's son*
JADE MAID, *Zhang's daughter*
RUNNER
BAO ZHENG, *Prefect of Kaifeng*
YAN SHUANGMEI, *a Taoist priest*
ATTENDANTS

ACT I

(Enter Lu Zhailang with his servant Zhang Qian.)

LU:

Chief of the rakes,
Unrivalled among rogues,
Feared by the townsfolk—
A powerful bully!

I am Lu Zhailang. Now the empire is at peace under our sovereign's sagacious rule. After I had served at court for several years His Majesty graciously transferred me here. I will not take a small official post, just as I scorn to ride a hack. I associate with idlers and rowdies, swindlers and thieves, passing my time every day in the street or with my hawk and hounds. When others have rarities or pictures which I have not, I borrow them for three days and return them on the fourth. When they have good horses or fine saddles, I use them for three days and give them back on the fourth, none the worse for wear, for I am a decent fellow. After coming to Xuzhou from the capital, I was ambling down the street one day when I noticed a fine woman in a silversmith's shop. I wanted to take a good look, but my horse was going too fast for me to have time. Have you found out who she is, Zhang Qian?

ZHANG:

Knowing you were interested, sir, I made inquiries.

LU:

What is her family?

ZHANG:

She is the wife of a silversmith named Li Si, a fine figure of a woman—pretty as a picture.

LU:

How can I get hold of her?

ZHANG:

It shouldn't be difficult, sir. We'll take a silver kettle to his shop to be mended, give him a good sum of money and some cups of wine, and get his wife to drink too. Then grab her to horse, and we're off!

With the silver kettle as our excuse,
We'll seize the woman and make off!

LU:

A magnificent idea! Saddle my horse today, and come with me to the silversmith to have that kettle mended. *(Exeunt.) (Enter Li Si with his wife and children)*

LI:

All is settled by fate: It is useless to toil and moil. I am a native of Xuzhou named Li Si. I have a wife whose maiden name is Zhang, who has borne me two children. My son is called Happy Boy, and my daughter Sweet Maid. I make a living as a silversmith. I am just opening shop for the day. Is anyone coming? *(Enter Lu with Zhang Qian.)*

LU:

Because Li Si's wife is a charmer,
I have followed Zhang Qian here.

I am Lu Zhailang. This kettle had a fall and started leaking, so I am taking it to the silversmith to be mended. Here we are at the door. Take my horse, boy, and fetch me a seat.

ZHANG:

Very good, sir.

LU *(sitting down):*

Call the silversmith out, Zhang Qian.

ZHANG:

Yes, sir. *(Calling)* Here, silversmith! His Honour Lu Zhailang is at the door calling you.

(Li Si comes out and kneels down fearfully)

LI:

>What are your commands, sir?

LU:

>Are you the silversmith?

LI:

>Yes, sir.

LU:

>Don't be afraid, Li Si. I have nothing against you. Get up.

LI:

>What can I do for Your Honour?

LU:

>This silver kettle of mine has been knocked down and broken. If you mend it for me, I'll give you ten silver taels.

LI:

>That is easy. I dare not ask for so much money.

LU:

>You are a poor man, how could I take advantage of you? Make a good job of it. Here is some silver to buy wine.
>*(Li takes the kettle and mends it.)*

LI:

>Now it is as good as new. It's ready. Please look, sir.

LU:

>Clever rascal—it really is as good as new. Zhang Qian, have you got wine there?

ZHANG:

>Yes, sir.

LU:

>Give him a few cups as a reward.
>*(Wine is poured out, and Li Si has three cups)*

LI:
>I have had enough.

LU:
>How large is your family?

LI:
>There is my humble wife. I will call her out to pay her respects. Wife! Come and pay your respects to His Honour.
>*(Li's Wife comes out to curtsey to Lu.)*

LU:
>A fine woman! Give her three cups of wine. I will drink a cup too, and so shall you, Zhang Qian. Well, Li Si, these three cups of wine seal our agreement. The silver is for you, and I am taking your wife with me to Zhengzhou. Don't you dare go to the yamen to sue me! *(Exit with Li's Wife.)*

LI *(shedding tears):*
>In broad daylight and time of peace, he has made off with my wife! I can't let him get away with that! Let me go and lay a charge against him in some yamen. *(Exit.) (Enter Zhang Gui's Wife with her son and daughter)*

ZHANG'S WIFE:
>*A flower may blossom again,*
>*But youth never returns.*
>My maiden name is Li. My husband's name is Zhang, and he is a clerk in Zhengzhou yamen. We are a family of four, with a son called Golden Boy and a daughter called Jade Maid. My husband is at his office, but he should be back soon. *(Enter Li Si.)*

LI:
>*I run like an arrow,*
>*As if my feet had wings.*
>I am Li Si. I have come to Zhengzhou after Lu Zhailang, because he carried off my wife. I intend to charge him, but don't know where the yamen is. Here I am in the main street. Help!

What is this pain in my heart? I am dying! Who will save me?
(Enter Zhang Gui with a Runner)

ZHANG:

I am Zhang Gui, a native of Zhengzhou. After studying the Confucian classics in my youth, I found an official post. There are four of us in my family. My wife is the daughter of a physician named Li from Huazhou, and we have two children—Golden Boy and Jade Maid. I am a clerk in Zhengzhou yamen. As there is no work in the office today, I am going home. I see a crowd. Go and find out what has happened, man.

RUNNER *(to Li Si)*:

Who are you? Why are you lying on the ground?

LI:

I have had a heart attack and am dying. Have pity on me, brother, and save me!

RUNNER *(to Zhang)*:

There is a man on the ground having a heart attack.

ZHANG:

Let me have a look. Hey, you! Why are you lying there?

LI:

I have had a heart attack and am dying. Save me, sir!

ZHANG:

Good deeds bring their reward of happiness. My wife knows how to treat heart attacks. Why not take him home and give him a cordial? *(To the Runner)* Help him to my house, man. Here we are. Where are you, wife?

ZHANG'S WIFE *(greeting her husband)*:

So you're back. Let me get you some tea and food.

ZHANG:

Not just yet. When I was passing the Lion, I found a man having a heart attack, and I have brought him home. Prepare a cordial for him and you'll save his life. Good deeds bring their reward of happiness.

ZHANG'S WIFE:

I'll go and brew a cordial now. *(She prepares the medicine)* Drink this, sir.

LI *(taking it):*

Ah, this cordial has restored me. Thank you from the bottom of my heart! If not for you both, I should have died.

ZHANG:

May I ask where you are from, sir? What is your name?

LI:

My name is Li, and as I am the fourth in my family they call me Li Si. I am from Xuzhou, a silversmith by trade.

ZHANG'S WIFE:

Since your name is Li and my maiden name is Li too, I would like you to be my brother. Let me see if my husband is willing. *(To Zhang.)* As this gentleman and I are both named Li, I would like to call him my brother if you are willing.

ZHANG:

Just as you like. Come here, Li Si. My wife wants you to be her brother. What do you say?

LI:

You have saved my life. I would gladly work in your house as a stable-boy, let alone be your wife's brother.

ZHANG:

Very well, now you are my brother-in-law and my wife is your sister. But what brought you to this district, brother?

LI:

    Someone has done me a great wrong. Now that you are my sister and brother-in-law, you must help me.

ZHANG:

    Who has wronged you? I'll have him arrested. Everybody knows me here!

LI:

    It was Lu Zhailang, who has carried off my wife. You must help me!

ZHANG *(clapping his hand to his mouth)*:

    Heavens, what a shock you gave me! It is lucky for you you are here. If you had said that anywhere else, you wouldn't have lived to tell the tale. I'll give you some money for your journey back to Xuzhou, brother, but don't mention that name again.

> *The man you accuse has great power,*
> *While you, the plaintiff, have none;*
> *No matter how plausible you are,*
> *What court dares issue a warrant?*
> *The sound of his name will strike terror into them.*
> *You had better not quarrel with him,*
> *But swallow your anger,*
> *And find an ugly wife*
> *Who will not cause trouble.*
> *Lu is high-handed as Heaven,*
> *An officer who overrides the law*
> *And will even threaten government offices,*
> *Seizing men's wives and daughters*
> *And trampling upon honest citizens.*
> *Few officials have such power!*
> *(Exit.)*

LI:

    As I cannot charge him here, I will go back to Xuzhou.
(Exit)

    (Enter Lu Zhailang)

LU:

I am Lu Zhailang. I took Li Si's wife from him in Xuzhou, and at first I loved her as my own life, but now I cannot stand the sight of her. Here I am in Zhengzhou. It is the Spring Festival, when everyone sacrifices to the ancestral graves. There must be some good-looking women among these crowds. I will take Zhang Qian and my other men out to enjoy the fine weather in the country. *(Exit.)*

(Enter Zhang Gui, leading his wife.)

ZHANG:

I am Zhang Gui. This is the Spring Festival, when each family sacrifices to the ancestral graves, and I am taking my wife to our graveyard. We government officers are usually a bad lot. It takes some doing to get these positions of ours.

A clerk such as I has great authority,
We have charge of all government files,
And if we sue a man,
We know many devices
To make things hot for him.
We never do a good turn
But try to ruin men,
Squeezing their money out of them
For ourselves.
When we have some information
We make out warrants with fiery haste
And summon the accused as quickly as smoke;
When the runners drag them to court
We feel as if some beautiful girl
Were coming to the painted hall
Amid singing and fluting.
We embezzle state funds,
Grind the faces of the poor,
Throw parents into gaol,
Make wives and children suffer hunger and cold.
We stay away from home for weeks on end,
Spending our time with singsong girls in brothels,

Storing up wealth, living in luxury,
Amassing property and buying land:
A few thousand peach and apricot trees,
And every leaf or twig a tale of injustice!
We part men from their silver
So that we can wear ornaments of gold;
We force them to sell their old houses
So that we can live in new mansions.
When our term of office is over
And we await new appointments,
The Ministry of Justice goes through our files;
Then we are fettered and fined,
Made to sell our luxurious estates;
And when the people see we have lost power,
They come down on us like a whirlwind
Which drives all clouds before it;
We are sent into exile hundreds of miles from home,
Or made to do hard labour for a year,
And have to pant for breath!

Here we are at the graveyard. How lovely the country looks in spring!

Laughter is heard all over the countryside,
Fresh soil is added to the mouldering graves;
Men remember their dead and mourn them.
On one side golden orioles sing,
On the other mortal men shed bitter tears;
Birds warble in the tender willows,
While human beings weep before ancient tombs.

ZHANG'S WIFE:

Let us stay here a little, husband.
(Enter Lu Zhailang with his men.)

LU:

Come for a stroll with me. Here is a fine graveyard, with an oriole on a tree. Give me my catapult. *(He aims at the bird.)*

GOLDEN BOY *(crying):*

Mother, my head is broken!

ZHANG'S WIFE:

What young donkey has hit my child with his dirty catapult?

ZHANG:

How dare a lout shoot into our family graveyard? Don't you know who I am? Let me see who is there!
Who is the wretch outside the wall?
I hurry forward to see.

LU:

Who do you think you are dressing down, Zhang Gui?

ZHANG:

I fall back a step in terror!

LU:

Are you looking for trouble, you scoundrel? Who do you think I am? How dare you abuse me?

ZHANG:

I feel like a man
Who walks over a precipice,
Trembling in panic,
Expecting death any moment!
I came out to celebrate the Spring Festival,
And to sacrifice at my ancestral graves;
We were drinking, laughing and chatting,
When he drew his catapult,
And his shot flew past my eyes!

LU:

You're going to beat me, are you, Zhang Gui? Do you want to be killed?

ZHANG:

I do not know how to answer.

ZHANG'S WIFE:

What silly boy has broken my darling's head?

ZHANG:

Don't talk so loudly and so foolishly!

GOLDEN BOY:

He's cut my head open!

ZHANG:

You little simpleton,
You don't know the meaning of worry!
I am out of my mind with terror...
And have no idea what to say;
But I dare delay no longer,
And step forward holding my gown,
Prepared to eat dirt. (He kneels before Lu.)

LU:

How dare you swear at me, Zhang Gui? Don't you know me? Take a look. Damn you, you shall suffer for this!

ZHANG:

I had no idea it was Your Honour. I would rather have died than speak to you like that.

LU:

Well, well. Even a gentleman may say one wrong word in a thousand, while even a low brute may say one right. He had no idea it was me. If he had known, of course he would not have dared. I won't take offence then. Whose graveyard is this?

ZHANG:

It is my family graveyard.

LU:

You might ask me in to rest for a while in that case.
Then even your ancestors' spirits will go to heaven.

ZHANG:

Please come inside, Your Honour.

LU:

A fine place. Who is that woman I hear speaking?

ZHANG:

That is my wife.

LU:

You might ask her to greet me.

ZHANG:

Wife, come and pay your respects to His Honour.

ZHANG'S WIFE:

Why should I?

ZHANG:

Do as I tell you.
(Zhang's Wife curtseys to Lu.)

LU *(bowing in return)*:

A charming woman I To think he has a wife like that, and I haven't. Damn you, Zhang Gui! How dare you swear at me? I'm not going to let you off lightly.

Come here and listen to me. Bring your wife to my house first thing tomorrow. If you don't turn up, you will pay double for it. Bring me my horse. I am going now. *(Exit.)*

ZHANG'S WIFE:

Who is he, husband? Why are you so afraid of him?

ZHANG:

Let's pack up, wife, and go home.
Trouble lurks in your charming smile,
Grief comes of your beautiful eyes;

For these years my luck has been bad,
And there is no one to help me.
I am a goose with its head cut off,
A worm writhing on hot ground.
His whispered order by his horse
Is like the emperor's edict.
(He picks up the catapult pellet and bows)
This shot served as a go-between,
Coming like a bolt from the blue.
You will have a wife tomorrow,
But I shall have none.
(Exeunt.)

ACT II

(Enter Lu Zhailang with Zhang Qian.)

LU:

When you plant flowers they may not bloom,
But a willow slip may grow to give shade.

I am Lu Zhailang. When I went out to enjoy the countryside in spring, in Zhang Gui's graveyard I saw an oriole on a tree, and drew my catapult. My shot went wide and hit Zhang Gui's child. He abused me roundly and I wanted to kill him, till I saw he had a pretty wife. Then I told him he need not give her to me at once, but could send her to me the next day. I have not slept all night. If he is late, I shall kill him. Go to the door, Zhang Qian, and keep a lookout. Let me know when he comes. *(Enter Zhang with his wife.)*

ZHANG:

Hurry, wife!

ZHANG'S WIFE:

It is barely dawn. Are you out of your mind? Where are you taking me?

ZHANG:

There is a wedding in my aunt's house in East Village. We mustn't be late. Let's walk faster. You go first, wife.

(Zhang's Wife walks in front.)

ZHANG:

What can I do? His Honour Lu Zhailang said: "Zhang Gui, bring your wife to my house first thing tomorrow." If I do not take her, he will kill me. If I take her, the two children will cry for their mother and that will kill me too. What can I do?

He has lost all human feeling:
Relying on his roughs,
He cruelly drags a mother from her children
And tears husband and wife apart.

Sun and moon may be eclipsed,
But how can a husband give away his wife?
Yet today I am acting as the go-between,
And must bring wedding gifts,
While the bridegroom sends
Neither sheep, nor wine, nor silk.
Powerful and ruthless,
He fears no divine retribution.
All is dark, I am utterly lost!
I can no longer distinguish
Between joy and anger,
Between high and low.
My wife is being taken,
My family is ruined;
But I dare not tell her,
As I stumble on.
You are Lady Yu[8]
Bidding farewell to her lord,
I am Fan Li[9]
Presenting the beauty to the king;
You are Wang Zhaojun[10]
Married to the Hunnish Khan;
You are young,
With a son and daughter;
We lived free from worries and cares,
Till out of a clear sky

---

[8] The favourite of Xiang Yu, who contended with Liu Bang for the empire at the end of the Qin Dynasty but was defeated. Before Xiang Yu went into battle for the last time, Lady Yu bade him a touching farewell.

[9] Minister of the King of Yue, who fought against the Kingdom of Wu during the Warring States Period. To make the King of Wu forget affairs of state, Fan Li presented him with the celebrated beauty Xi Shi.

[10] A beautiful court lady of the Han Dynasty. Legend has it that she Was given in marriage to a Hunnish Khan to win the friendship of the Huns.

This storm arose;
Now our family is scattered
Like broken tiles!

ZHANG'S WIFE:

We have been walking for some time. Where are we?

ZHANG:

We have arrived.

ZHANG'S WIFE:

Is this the house? What business are they in to own such a big place?

ZHANG:

The morning sun shines upon quiet pavilions,
The spring breeze penetrates the gauzy curtains—
Happy the owner of such a property!
This man steals money,
Snatches other men's wives;
This is the brigand's castle,
And there flies his flag,
As if he were an outlaw of Liangshan[11]

Wait here, wife. *(He greets Zhang Qian.)* Brother, please announce that Zhang Gui is at the gate.

ZHANG QIAN:

At last! You deserve to die for this delay. Wait here while I announce you.

LU:

What is that fellow there?

ZHANG QIAN:

Zhang Gui and his wife are at the gate.

---

[11] Headquarters of the peasant revolt during the Song Dynasty, described in the famous novel *Outlaws of the Marsh*

LU:

    I'll not stop to change, Zhang Qian. Show them in.
(Zhang and his wife bow to Lu.)

LU:

    You are late, Zhang Gui.

ZHANG:

    I waited till the two children were asleep, then made ready and hurried here. So it is after dawn.

LU:

    Never mind. Is that your wife? Come here and let me see you. A fine woman, more beautiful than when I saw her yesterday. I thank you! Bring the wine and we will have three cups.

ZHANG:

    I gulp down the heady wine.

ZHANG'S WIFE:

    Don't drink too much, husband. I'm afraid you will get drunk.

ZHANG:

    She's afraid I may get drunk
And may be cheated.
I turn to suppress a sigh!
I want to get dead-drunk,
To be dead to the world,
So as not to remember our parting.

ZHANG'S WIFE:

    Tell me, husband, why do you look so sad?

ZHANG:

    To tell the truth, wife, His Honour wants you as his mistress. That is why I have brought you here.

ZHANG'S WIFE:

Husband! How can you be so cruel!

LU:

Stop talking. Go and change your clothes in the inner-room.

ZHANG'S WIFE:

Husband, you have broken my heart!

ZHANG:

My heart is broken too, wife.

LU:

Are you feeling sad, Zhang Gui? Unwilling to leave her?

ZHANG:

How dare I be, Your Honour! But I have a son and daughter at home with no one to look after them.

LU:

Why didn't you say so before? So you have two children at home with no one to look after them. *(He calls Zhang Qian.)* Zhang Qian, tell Li Si's wife to get dressed, and give her to Zhang Gui.

ZHANG QIAN:

Yes, sir.

LU:

Since your two children need someone to look after them, Zhang Gui, I will give you my sister Jiao E. You have given me your wife, and you shall have my sister in exchange. If you swear at her or beat her when you are drunk, it will be like swearing at me or beating me. I entrust this girl to you. Now I am going to the inner chamber. *(Exit.)*

ZHANG:

What shall I do now? Ah!

*He has seized my wife
And given me another;
I have thrown away a sweet peach
For a sour pear.
Surely she is no sister of his!
I am ushered down the steps,
Past the screen and out of the gate;
And turn to look back at my wife,
At my good helpmate,
As if we were husband and wife
In a former life.
I must sleep alone for the rest of my days,
And never see her again except in dreams. (Exit.)*

ACT III

(Enter Li Si.)

LI:

I am Li Si. Because Lu Zhailang snatched my wife I went to Zhengzhou to sue him, but finding that impossible, I came back to Xuzhou. Now my children have disappeared, so I cannot stay here either. I will go back to Zhengzhou to my sister and brother-in-law. *(Exit.) (Enter Zhang Gui's two children!)*

GOLDEN BOY:

I am Zhang Gui's son, Golden Boy. This is my sister, Jade Maid. Our father and mother are out visiting. They should be back soon. *(Enter Zhang Gui.)*

ZHANG:

Ah, was ever any man as unhappy as I? Here I am back at home, but what shall I say to my children? You brute, Lu Zhailang!

Relying on his roughs,
This lecher tramples on good citizens.
Who is bold enough to pick a quarrel with him?
He takes whatever woman strikes his fancy,
With no regard for her husband,
And flouts morality—
But who dares stand against him?
Though there is a court of justice for civilians,
A military court for the army,
They are useless.
Now the mother is torn from her children,
And the husband and wife
Who shared so many hardships
Can never meet again. Well, here I am home.

GOLDEN BOY:

Father, you are back! Where is mother?

ZHANG:

> She will be home soon, child. Ah, what shall I do?
> *I wish I could banish sad thoughts,*
> *But how can I hide my sighs?*

GOLDEN BOY:

> Why hasn't mother come?

ZHANG:

> *She may have gone up the mountain*
> *And turned into stone.*
> *I pat my son's head*
> *And hold my daughter's hand.*
> *Ah, children, this is a sad day!*

GOLDEN BOY:

> Father, where is mother truly?

ZHANG:

> Your mother has been carried off by Lu Zhailang.

GOLDEN BOY:

> How dare he! I could burst with rage!
> *(He faints.)*

ZHANG *(reviving him):*

> Wake up, child. Poor little creatures!
> *(Enter Zhang Qian with Li's Wife)*

ZHANG QIAN:

> I am *Zhang* Qian. By my master's order, I have brought this lady here. Is Zhang Gui in?

ZHANG:

> Who is that calling outside? Let me open the gate and see. *(He opens the gate.)* Ah, what are you doing here?

ZHANG QIAN:

His Honour ordered me to bring you this lady. Say no more, and don't you say anything either, ma'am. I am going. *(Exit)*

ZHANG:

Please come in, ma'am. Children, come and pay your respects to your stepmother. These are my former wife's two children, ma'am. I hope you will take good care of them.

LI'S WIFE:

Rest assured, sir, I shall do my best for them.

ZHANG:

Take good care of these children,
These two unfortunates.
Even if you treat them kindly,
Not cruelly—

LI'S WIFE:

Make your mind easy. I shall look after them as if they were my own.

ZHANG:

Even if you treasure them
Like pearls or jewels,
You will not be like their own mother.
(Enter Li Si.)

LI:

I have come back to Zhengzhou. Here is my sister and brother-in-law's house. I'll call at the gate. *(He calls.)*

ZHANG:

There is someone at the gate, ma'am. I'll just see who it is. *(He sees Li.)* So it is my brother-in-law. I am suffering from the same trouble as you.

LI:

My sister has a good cure for it.

ZHANG:

    Not that trouble. Your sister has been snatched by Lu Zhailang too.

LI:

    So, Lu Zhailang, you owe us two women!

ZHANG:

    I am better off than you, brother. He gave me a woman in exchange.

LI:

    Ha, Lu Zhailang, when you took my wife you didn't give me so much as a hen. Since my sister has gone, brother, I had better go back to Xuzhou.

ZHANG:

    Your new sister is here, brother. Why not let me introduce her?

LI:

    I will just greet her and then I must go. Don't try to keep me, brother. *(He sees his wife.)*

ZHANG:

    Must you really go back now, brother?

LI:

    I think I'd like to stay here after all.

ZHANG:

> Strange! *The two of them*
> *Are exchanging significant glances,*
> *There is some mystery here.*
> *One looks at a loss,*
> *The other is hiding some secret;*
> *Their expressions are most suspicious.*
> *(Enter a Runner)*

RUNNER:

You are wanted to write out a document, Secretary Zhang.

ZHANG:

Stay here with your sister, brother, while I go to the office to write out a document. *(Exit.)*
(Li Si and his wife clasp each other and weep)

LI:

Wife, I have missed you so much!
(Enter the children)

GOLDEN BOY:

Where has father gone, mother?

LI'S WIFE:

He has gone to his office to write a document.

GOLDEN BOY:

Then we will go to look for him.
(He and his sister go out.)

LI and WIFE:

I have missed you so much!
(Zhang rushes in and sees them together. Li Si and his wife kneel down)

ZHANG:

So they admit their guilt!
A gentleman should not be false,
Yet my brother has betrayed me—
What if others did this to you?
I was your sister's husband,
But you have taken her from me,
You, whom I cured of your illness,
Whom I supported
And took as my relative.
As soon as I left the house

79

You stole my wife.
What wrong have I done you, pray?
You are not like that friend
Who shared his gold,
But like the fellow
Who chopped off his comrade's feet.
Now friends have turned to foes,
The guest has become the host;
The hearts of some men are wicked!
He snatched your wife,
You dared not take revenge,
But instead you make love to my wife,
Here in my house!

LI:

Let me tell you the truth, brother. This is my wife. Lu Zhailang lied when he told you she was his sister and gave her to you.

ZHANG:

That is what you say.
Who believes your wicked lies?
I must get to the bottom of this—
A fine way to carry on!
You make no difference between weak and strong,
Between friend and foe, right and wrong.
Even if you are husband and wife
Who have come together again,
You have utterly destroyed my family.
Where are my two children?

LI'S WIFE:

When you went to your office they went after you.

ZHANG:

So you have murdered my children. I am choking with rage!

In a moment of weakness

I made the wrong choice of a friend.
What have you done to deserve such happiness,
Leaving me to wail in misery alone?
You make love to another man's wife,
And what have you done with my children?

Well, well. My wife has been carried off by Lu Zhailang, my two children have disappeared, and this woman who was given me has turned out to be the silversmith's wife. How can I stay here? I'll leave you both my property, brother. See that I get enough food and clothing each month. I am going to be a Taoist priest in Huashan.

LI:

How can you leave your fine property and your farm, brother? I'll take hold of your clothes and stop you!

ZHANG:

Let go of my clothes!
Water and fire cannot remain together.

LI:

How can you give up all your land and jewels, brother?

ZHANG:

Say no more of my land and jewels.

LI:

Brother, I'll give you my wife!

ZHANG:

Pah!
Have you no sense of shame? You are married already.

LI'S WIFE:

Then give me a divorce certificate, sir.

ZHANG:

Why do you need a divorce certificate?

LI:

    So that when Lu Zhailang hears of this, he will not blame us.

ZHANG:

    Lu Zhailang is not my patron.

LI:

    I wonder where my sister is.

ZHANG:

    The drunken lord needs serving-maids,
    A pretty woman brings trouble to her husband;
    This dusty world is not worth lingering in;
    Better be a hermit in the mountains.

LI:

    How can you give up so much property, land and other valuables?

ZHANG:

    Do not ask who will be the steward
    When the master is gone.
    You have your wife again now.
    I have lost all interest
    In worldly fame or profit,
    In mortal wisdom or folly.
    Human affairs change like the floating clouds,
    Friendship is autumn grass which withers daily.
    In vain my tears stain the bamboo—
    I am old and disillusioned.

LI:

    I wonder where my sister is now.

ZHANG:

    Yes, indeed, your sister!
    Lu is listening to music,

> *Watching a woman dancing,*
> *With flutes and maids around him.*
> *The gold goblet is filled with wine,*
> *The embroidered screens are spread;*
> *He has the means*
> *To kidnap other men's wives,*
> *And to seduce married women.*

LI:

We can see to your food and clothing all the year round, brother. But how can you leave your home and bid farewell to your relatives and friends?

ZHANG:

> *I have resigned myself*
> *To be a hermit in the woods;*
> *I do not want to rival*
> *Brave men and heroes.*
> *It is not that I choose the mountains,*
> *But I have lost my children and sweet wife. (Exit.)*

LI:

So my brother-in-law has gone. I shall see to it that he is well supplied with food. Now I'll go to the inner chamber to drink with my wife to our happy reunion. *(Exeunt.)*

ACT IV

(Enter Prefect Bao with Attendants.)

BAO:

The court drums thunder,
The runners are ranged on two sides;
This is the judgement seat of the King of Hell,
To which all spirits are summoned. I am Bao Zheng, a native of Laoer Village in Luzhou. I hold the posts of Academician of Longtu Pavilion and Prefect of Kaifeng. Some years ago His Majesty ordered me to make a tour of inspection. In Xuzhou I found the son and daughter of the silversmith Li Si. As their mother had been abducted by Lu Zhailang and their father had disappeared, I kept them with me. In Zhengzhou I found another boy and girl who were the children of the clerk Zhang Gui. As their mother had also been abducted by Lu Zhailang and their father had disappeared, I kept them too and made them study. Now, ten years later, the young men have passed the examinations and taken up official posts. I bore these facts in mind, well aware that Lu was oppressing innocent people, kidnapping women and committing all manner of crimes. Then I reported to His Majesty that a man named Yu Qiji[12] had been injuring good citizens, abducting women and breaking the law time and again. His Majesty was angry and issued an order for his execution. The next day, when the emperor asked for Lu, I told him: "He has been killed for his crimes." The emperor was shocked. "How could you kill him?" he asked. "As he oppressed the people and kidnapped women, Your Majesty sentenced him to death," I said. "Now he has been executed." The emperor could hardly believe his ears. "Show me the decree," he said. Then he found the name Yu Qiji changed to Lu Zhailang, and read: "The felon Lu Zhailang, who oppressed the people, is to be executed." By this trick I had Lu Zhailang killed, and rid the people of a tyrant. But the silversmith

---

[12] In Chinese Lu Zhailang and Yu Qiji look very similar.

Li Si and the clerk Zhang Gui are still missing. I have told their sons to take their sisters to temples all over the country to offer sacrifice, hoping that in this way they may find their parents. If I can reunite their families, I shall have done a good deed. Today the two young men have taken their sisters to sacrifice at the Yuntai Taoist Temple. I will follow them there.

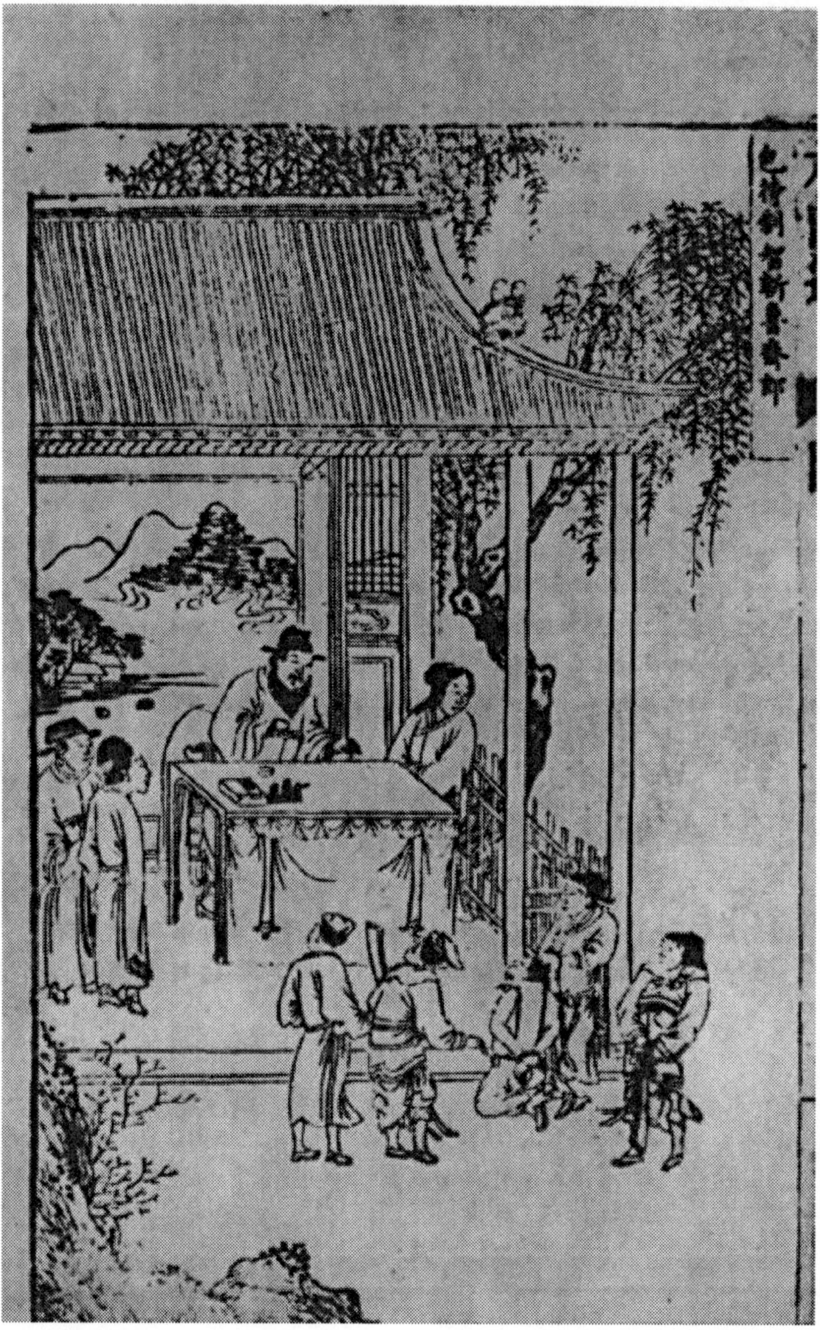
包待制智斬魯齋郎

Lu Zhailang flouted the law,
And abducted other men's wives;
By writing his name as Yu Qiji,
I succeeded in having him killed. (Exit.)
(Enter Yan Shuangmei, a Taoist priest.)

YAN:

The way that can be told is not the invariable way.
The names that can be named are not invariable names.[13]

I am Yan Shuangmei, a priest in Yuntai Temple here. Today I have no duties. I will see if anyone is coming.
(Enter Li Si and his wife.)

LI:

I am Li Si. Since I lost my children ten years have passed, and I do not know whether they are alive or dead. I have come to Yuntai Temple today to sacrifice for my sister and brother-in-law and their two children. *(He greets the priest.)*

Good day, priest. I am from Xuzhou and have come here to offer sacrifice.

YAN:

For whom is this sacrifice?

LI:

For my brother-in-law, Zhang Gui, and his wife and two children. Here are five taels of silver for you for chanting the holy canons.

YAN:

We priests have no use for money, but I will accept it for the moment and get you some food. Here is someone else coming.
(Enter Zhang's Wife, dressed as a nun.)

---

[13] A quotation from the Taoist classic, the *Dao De Jing*.

ZHANG'S WIFE:

I am Chang Gui's wife. I was seized by Lu Zhailang ten years ago. My two children have disappeared and I do not know whether my husband is alive or dead. When Lu Zhailang was executed by Prefect Bao, I renounced the world and became a nun. Today I am going to Yuntai Temple to offer a sacrifice for Zhang Gui. Here I am. *(She greets the priest.)*

YAN:

Ah, a nun! Where are you from?

ZHANG'S WIFE:

I have come to offer a sacrifice for my husband Zhang Gui and my children.

LI:

Who is offering a sacrifice for Zhang Gui?

ZHANG'S WIFE:

I am.

LI:

Aren't you my sister? *(He greets her, weeping)*

ZHANG'S WIFE:

Who is this lady, brother?

LI:

That is my wife. How did you escape, sister?

ZHANG'S WIFE:

When Prefect Bao had Lu Zhailang executed, I was able to leave his house. So today I have come to Yuntai Temple to sacrifice for your brother-in-law and my children.

LI:

I have come for the same purpose. Let us sacrifice together. But see, some others are coming. *(Enter Li's son and daughter.)*

HAPPY BOY:

I am Happy Boy and this is my sister Sweet Maid. Our mother was carried off by Lu Zhailang and our father has disappeared. Luckily for us, Prefect Bao kept us and brought us up. Now I have passed the examinations and come first in the palace test. The prefect told us to go to Yuntai Temple to offer a sacrifice for our parents. Here we are. Good day, priest.

YAN:

If I had known a gentleman was coming, I would have gone out to welcome you. Please excuse me. What can I do for you and this young lady?

HAPPY BOY:

We have come to offer a sacrifice.

YAN:

For whom?

HAPPY BOY:

For my father, Li Si, the silversmith.

LI:

Who is talking about Li Si?

HAPPY BOY:

Isn't that my father?

LI:

Who are you?

HAPPY BOY:

I am your son, Happy Boy, and this is my sister, Sweet Maid.

LI'S WIFE:

Ah, children, where have you been?
(Li's son and daughter weep and speak of the past.)

LI:

    Now, children, pay your respects to your aunt.
(They bow to Zhang's Wife.)

ZHANG'S WIFE:

    Who are these?

LI:

    They are my children.

ZHANG'S WIFE *(weeping)***:**

    Now your family is reunited, but I do not know where my husband and children are. *(Enter Zhang's son and daughter.)*

GOLDEN BOY:

    I am Zhang Gui's son, Golden Boy, and this is my sister, Jade Maid. My mother was carried off by Lu Zhailang and my father has disappeared. Luckily for us, Prefect Bao kept us and brought us up. I have passed the examinations and become an official. The prefect told us to go to Yuntai Temple to sacrifice for our father. Here we are.

YAN:

    Here is another young gentleman, who has brought a young lady too. What brings you here, sir?

GOLDEN BOY:

    We have come to offer a sacrifice.

YAN:

    For whom?

GOLDEN BOY:

    For my father, Zhang Gui, and my mother.

ZHANG'S WIFE:

    Who is talking about Zhang Gui?

GOLDEN BOY:

I am.

ZHANG'S WIFE:

Can you be Golden Boy?

GOLDEN BOY:

Sister, isn't this our mother?
(They weep.)

ZHANG'S WIFE:

Where have you been during the last ten years?

GOLDEN BOY:

After you left, our father disappeared too. Then luckily for us, Prefect Bao brought us up, and I have passed the examinations and been appointed to an official post. Prefect Bao told us to come to Yuntai Temple to sacrifice for our parents. We never thought to meet you here, mother. I wonder if our father is alive too. *(He weeps)*

LI:

If this is your son, sister, let me give him my daughter, Sweet Maid, as his wife.

GOLDEN BOY:

Mother, give my sister, Jade Maid, to your nephew as his wife.

ZHANG'S WIFE:

Now our two families are reunited. I only wonder where Zhang Gui is. *(Enter Zhang Gui with a clapper)*

ZHANG:

> *In a patched sheepskin,*
> *I beg for food when hungry;*
> *Tough I cannot be an immortal,*
> *I avoid the needless troubles of the world.*
> *Suddenly my servant-lad reports*

That a fog has shut out the sun;
Wood-cutters clap their hands and laugh,
Snow falls over the winter plum
And whirls in the wind like blossoms,
Scattering in the air like feathers.
Now the village wine goes up in price,
Travellers slip on the ice,
In bitter cold the swallows' nests are frozen—
Can I cross the slippery bridge?
The poet cannot ride his donkey,
The scholar is barred from the pass,
The mountains are white with dark clouds above,
And the green hills seem covered with powder.
We hermits lead a quiet life!
In the world of men
Troubles arise from nothing,
But I rest and take my leisure like Xie An,[14]
Trying, like Lu Weng,[15] *to make the philosopher's stone,*
Wise as Xiao He, the law-maker,[16]
I drink, dance and sing with abandon,
For I have seen through worldly vanity.
Men hurry after fame and profit,
Busy with petty affairs,
While I lie and dream in peace,
Not envying noble rank or splendid mansions.
Happy the hermit's life the whole year round!
Here I pass spring and summer,
Autumn and winter,
By the fountains in the woods,
Resting at night in the mountain.
If you ask how I pass the time,

---

[14] A statesman and scholar of the Jin Dynasty.

[15] A famous alchemist of the Tang Dynasty.

[16] A minister of the first emperor of the Han Dynasty.

I seek the philosopher's stone
And practise yoga,
Laughing at the withered leaves
Which fall from the trees.
I remember when I drank with my wife
One Spring Festival in my ancestral graveyard;
We were a happy couple,
Not living in luxury,
But enjoying a carefree life,
With no need for silk or brocade....
But to speak of these things is as vain
As trying to catch fish up a tree.
Lu Zhailang was a reckless bully
Who had no respect for the law.

"Zhang Gui, bring me your wife," he said. "I want her." And I agreed.

It was not that I was a coward.
His head was struck off
By the executioner's sword,
But still I take my ease
On the mountain top.

I thought he would enjoy his wealth and noble rank for ever, but he was executed by Prefect Bao, and all the people rejoiced.

This proves that there is justice,
And all men praise the prefect,
For Bao Zheng is full of wisdom,
And Lu Zhailang was asking to be killed
When he seized other men's wives.
But now, as a hermit, I have found happiness.

Today I am going to enjoy myself at Yuntai Temple. Here I am.

ZHANG'S WIFE:

Li Si, look at that priest! He looks like your brother-in-law. Let me call him. Zhang Gui!

ZHANG *(turning)*:

Who is calling Zhang Gui? *(He sees her.* Isn't that my wife?

ZHANG'S WIFE:

Why have you left me and become a priest? You had better leave your holy orders now.

ZHANG:

When we parted
It was against my will,
I was then your heart-broken husband;
But after all these years
Our love is over.
You want me back now, but—
Our case is settled,
It cannot be reversed.

ZHANG'S WIFE and LI:

Give up your holy orders!

ZHANG:

I am already a priest. How can I turn back?
(Zhang's Wife, Li Si and Li's Wife all plead with him.)

ZHANG:

There is no need for all this clamour,
All this bowing and begging.

LI:

Brother, now our two families are reunited, how can you go away? You must do as I ask and give up your priesthood.

ZHANG:

I will not listen to such talk
Though you buzz about me like a swarm of bees
And your words are sweet as honey—
I shall not give up my orders.

95

ZHANG'S WIFE:

    You are used to comfort, husband. How can you be a priest? How can you stand such a hard life?

ZHANG:

> *You ask me why I choose this lonely life?*
> *It is my wish to go where fate directs me,*
> *To close my eyes when it is time to sleep,*
> *To lie down when I need rest.*
> *It is not that I want to leave you,*
> *But a man may just as well drift*
> *And laugh at the whole of creation;*
> *Husband and wife may part*
> *And give no thought to their children.*
> *Here I live free from care,*
> *Drinking as the fancy takes me,*
> *And sleep when drunk among the pines and creepers,*
> *Like the ancient philosopher*
> *Who sang at his wife's death*[17]
> *The world may think I am mad,*
> *But I will not trouble myself with mundane affairs;*
> *I will not frown,*
> *But sleep peacefully by the window. (Enter Bao Zheng)*

BAO:

    Events may surprise us, but there is a reason for every thing. I am Bao Zheng. I have come to Yuntai Temple and I see some people having a heated discussion. I wonder what has happened.

---

[17] When Zhuang Zhou's wife died, a friend who came to offer condolences found the philosopher singing and beating a basin.

LI:

Your Honour, I am the silversmith, Li Si. My sister was carried off by Lu Zhailang. Now my brother-in-law Zhang Gui has become a priest and will not recognize her as his wife.

BAO:

Why won't you recognize her as your wife, Zhang Gui?

ZHANG:

My two children have disappeared, and I have become a priest. Why then should I take a wife?

BAO:

Zhang Gui, your children are here before me, and Li Si's children too. Come here, all of you. Let Li Si's daughter marry Zhang Gui's son, and Zhang Gui's daughter marry Li Si's son, to link your two households in marriage. And let Zhang Gui return to his family. For there is no greater happiness in the world than family reunions. Let us kill a sheep and heat wine to celebrate.

Lu Zhailang was a bully,
Who carried off other men's wives;
By cunning I had him killed,
Freeing the people from his tyranny.
Now husbands and wives have come together again:
Let your children marry each other.
To all of you the state has shown its favour:
The young men's names are on the golden list,
And both your families are reunited;
Then face the north and thank His Majesty!
(THE END)

THE BUTTERFLY DREAM

CHARACTERS
WANG
WANG'S WIFE
BIG WANG, *Wang's eldest son*
MIDDLE WANG, *Wang's second son*
LITTLE WANG, *Wang's third son*
GE BIAO, *a local bully*
BAILIFF RUNNERS
BAO ZHENG, *Prefect of Kaifeng*
ZHANG QIAN, *his sergeant*
LI WAN, *another sergeant*
DONKEY ZHAO, *a horse thief*

ACT I

(Enter Wang, his wife and their three sons.)

WANG:

Comes the middle of the month, and the moon grows dim:
Comes middle age, and a man is good for nothing.

My name is Wang. I am a native of Zhongmou County in the prefecture of Kaifeng. There are five in my family. This is my wife, and we have three sons. They will not work on the land because they prefer to study. When will you show your worth, boys, and become famous?

BIG WANG:

What good is farming, father? When I have studied hard for ten years I shall become an official and make you all happy.

WANG and WIFE:

Good lad, good lad!

MIDDLE WANG:

I may study for ten years by. the window without receiving any recognition, father, but when I pass the examination and win fame, then the whole world will know me...

WANG and WIFE:

Good lad, good lad!

LITTLE WANG:

Father above and mother underneath....

WANG:

What's that? Why "mother underneath"?

LITTLE WANG:

When I was small I saw you in bed together, with mother underneath father.

WANG:

    You rascal!

LITTLE WANG:

    Father and mother, all I mean is that scholarship leads to a good career.

WANG:

    Good lad, good lad!

WIFE:

    Still, husband, you must find some way to set our boys up for life.

    Don't tell me scholarship leads to a good career—
We are short of money now.
What use is your hard study by the frosty window?
In this world rogues do better than honest men,
The clothes—not the men—are respected.
I always speak my mind:
What guarantee is there that our three sons
Will pass their test next spring?
How can they enter the dragon gate of officialdom?
(Exeunt!) (Enter Wang.)

WANG:

    I have come to the main street to buy paper and pens for the boys. Walking has tired me. Let me rest here. *(Enter Ge Biao.)*

GE:

    Generals and ministers come from common stock:
Men should carve out their own career.

    I am Ge Biao. Mine is a powerful family. When I kill men I do not have to pay with my life, but at most go to gaol for it. Today I am free, so I may as well take a ride. *(He knocks into Wang.)* Who is this old fellow who dares get in my horse's way? Beat the old ass! *(He beats and kills Wang.)* The old man is shamming dead in order to blackmail me. I'll let my horse kick and trample him. *(Exit.) (Enter the Bailiff.)*

BAILIFF:

> Big Wang, Middle Wang, Little Wang! Are you there?
> *(Enter the three sons.)*

SONS:

> What do you want?

BAILIFF:

> I am the bailiff. Somebody has killed your father in the street.

SONS:

> What! Mother, a fearful thing has happened! *(They weep)*

LITTLE WANG:

> Someone has killed our father! Mother, come here!

WIFE:

> What are you shouting about?

LITTLE WANG:

> Someone has killed our father.

WIFE:

> What! Never!
> *I puzzle my head over this terrible news,*
> *Running till I am out of breath*
> *And my voice is just a croak.*
> *I wish I had wings!*
> *What wrong had my husband done?*
> *When I catch his murderer*
> *I shall demand an answer.*
> *He never plotted with the enemy,*
> *Never harmed any man or the state.*
> *If my poor husband is really dead,*
> *I shall sue that wicked scoundrel.*
> *I run through the streets and market,*
> *Wiping my tears. (She sees the corpse)*

> *Look at those angry wounds!*
> *Here he lies, black and blue.*
> *So devoted a husband and father—*
> *Who could have thought you would die like this?*
> *None knows what will happen from one day to the next.*
> *Covered with blood,*
> *You lie here cold and limp,*
> *Your face like yellow paper.*
> *For an hour I call your name,*
> *But to my horror you will not wake;*
> *And you know how it is at home—*
> *How can we afford a sacrifice*
> *When we bury you tomorrow?*
> *All I have left is these three boys;*
> *It is true that a poor family has good sons.*

SONS:

Mother, they all say it was Ge Biao who killed our father. We are going to find him and take him to court, to make him pay with his life. *(Exeunt.)*

WIFE:

> *Ge Biao is a scholar of the Imperial College,*
> *Why should he strike a man dead?*
> *Now I must take the corpse home.*
> *He is an official and we are poor,*
> *Yet still I mean to sue him. (Enter Ge Biao.)*

GE:

I am Ge Biao. I have had a few cups of wine. Now there's nothing to do, I may as well go home. *(Enter Wang's three sons.)*

SONS:

There is the murderer! Catch him! *(They seize Ge.)* You beat our father to death!

GE:

What if I did? I am not afraid of you.

WIFE:

> *I shall charge you in the court!*
> *What does it matter if you are a noble,*
> *Related to the imperial house?*
> *Even the emperor's own sons and grandsons*
> *Must go to court for murder!*
> *(The three sons set on Ge Biao and kill him.)*

SONS:

This murderer is shamming drunk and won't get up.

WIFE:

Let me speak to him. *(To Ge.)* See here, what harm did my husband do you that you should beat him to death? And why should you sham drunk on the ground and refuse to get up? You can't escape like that! Get up, get up! Ah! Have you three killed him?

LITTLE WANG:

Lucky I didn't hit him!

WIFE:

> Now what shall we do?
> *You should have been more careful;*
> *What was the use of beating him like that?*
> *Although you did not pick a quarrel for nothing,*
> *And it was not wrong to kill him,*
> *You will have to go to court.*
> Your careers are ruined. *(She points to Ge's corpse.)*
> *You did not stop to think either*
> *That force would be met by force.*
> *Heaven is just and impartial,*
> *You acted the bully in the street*
> *And now you too lie here a bloody corpse.*
> *A general can be pierced by an arrow too,*
> *Though he likes to shoot at others.*

SONS:
> We have no money. How can we go to court?

WIFE:
> *Each day one ladle of soup, one single dish—*
> *How many spare chopsticks have we?*
> *We need money to go to court,*
> *But all we have to pawn is a few old books,*
> *And they will not bring us much.*
> *It must be your fate to die;*
> *But though you have killed a man*
> *You are good sons. (Enter the Runners.)*

RUNNERS:
> Don't let them get away! Catch those murderers!

WIFE:
> *Bitterness in my heart, tears in my eyes!*
> *Ruin has come down from Heaven!*
> *We are dragged away and cannot even protest.*
> *There lies my husband dead,*
> *And here before my eyes my sons are ruined;*
> *Good fortune never repeats itself,*
> *But troubles come thick and fast.*

RUNNERS:
> Murder is no small offence. Come to the court!

WIFE *(weeping):*
> Surely Heaven will not tolerate injustice.
> Evil must be repaid,
> And all men long for revenge,
> But alas! that the three of you should be involved,
> Three scholars about to pass the dragon gate
> And pluck the cassia bough.[18]

---

[18] A euphemism for passing the examination.

>   Because you took revenge
>   On your murdered father,
>   You will be arrested and tried,
>   Tortured with rack and thumbscrews;
>   I never knew that we were so ill-starred,
>   Never knew that you would kill him.
>   It was right to avenge your father;
>   Though you are executed
>   And go to the nether regions,
>   Your names will be remembered as filial sons.

RUNNERS:

>   Come to the court!

WIFE:

>   Now you have done this, boys, what shall we do?

SONS:

>   Ah, mother, what can we do?

WIFE:

>   *I made you study the classics and history,*
>   *As the mother of Mencius taught her son;*
>   *But your names will never appear on the golden list,*[19]
>   *Instead they will be in the list of felons!*
>   *Yet this was no premeditated murder,*
>   *And if punishment is decreed*
>   *At most only one of you should pay with his life—*
>   *How can all my sons be killed?*
>   *This will not be the end of our family. (Exeunt.)*

---

[19] Which announced the names of successful candidates in the examinations.

ACT II

(Enter Zhang Qian with Runners)

ZHANG:

All is ready to open court. *(Enter Bao Zheng.)*

BAO:

The court drums thunder,
The runners are ranged on two sides;
This is the judgement seat of the King of Hell,
To which all spirits are summoned.

I am Bao Zheng, a native of Laoer Village in Luzhou. I hold the posts of Academician of Longtu Pavilion and Prefect of Kaifeng. I am now going to preside over the morning session in my court. Zhang Qian, bring me whatever documents await my signature.

ZHANG:

Secretaries and clerks! Have you any documents for His Honour to sign? *(There is an answer off)*

ZHANG:

Why didn't you report this before? Your Honour, Suanzao County has sent us a horse thief, Donkey Zhao.

BAO:

Bring him in.
(The Runners bring in Donkey Zhao, who kneels before the prefect)

BAO:

Remove the cangue. You there, are you Donkey Zhao and did you steal horses?

DONKEY ZHAO:

Yes, Your Honour, I did.

BAO:

Zhang Qian, fasten the cangue on him and have him sent to the condemned cell, *(Donkey Zhao is led away)*

BAO:

I feel a little tired, Zhang Qian. Tell the secretaries to make no noise. I want to take a nap.

ZHANG:

Now, gentlemen, no noise! His Honour is resting. *(The prefect dozes off at the table)*

BAO *(talking in his sleep):*

Worried by affairs of state, how can I sleep? I have strolled to the back of the hall and found a small gate. Let me open it and have a look. What a beautiful garden! All the flowers are blooming in the warm spring weather. Set among the flowers is a pavilion, with a spider's web on it. A butterfly fluttering from the flowers is caught in the web. The sight makes me sad. Man may die at any hour, and even insects are exposed to danger. Ah, even insects have intelligence! A big butterfly has come to rescue the smaller. Ah, another butterfly has been caught in the web. No doubt the big butterfly will save it again.... How strange! The big butterfly is simply fluttering around the flowers. Instead of saving the smaller one, it has flown off. Well, as the sage said, all men have a sense of pity. Since it will not save the butterfly, let me do so. *(He makes a gesture as if releasing the butterfly.)*

ZHANG:

Your Honour, it is noon.

BAO *(waking):*

In my dream a butterfly's life
Was banging in the balance,
When I woke to hear Zhang Qian
Announcing that it is noon.
Well, Zhang Qian, are there any culprits awaiting trial? Send them in.

ZHANG:

Secretaries, are there any culprits awaiting trial? Send them in. *(There is a shout off.)*

ZHANG:

Your Honour, some felons have been sent from Zhongmou County. They are three brothers who beat the noble Ge Biao to death.

BAO:

How dare men of a small county kill a noble? Are they here?

ZHANG:

They are.

BAO:

Bring them into court, beating them.
(A Runner brings in the three sons and their mother!)

WIFE:

We are brought to this cruel yamen in Kaifeng,
Where the emperor's justice is administered.
Three scholars, who have not yet made their name,
Dragged here and tried as criminals.
Trembling and fearful,

112

Knowing our guilt,
We shall have to confess our crime.
This is not the county court;
Here in Kaifeng they are strict,
With none of our easy-going country ways.
The drum thunders beneath the steps;
Awe-struck and terrified,
I have lost my head and am utterly exhausted.
This is no light offence but a serious crime.
There my old man lies dead on the ground,
And here mother and sons are arrested.
My eyes shall see my own children executed.
I peep fearfully at this court
Which I never entered before.
Today our fate will be decided here,
The prefect will decide between right and wrong.
(She and her sons kneel before the prefect.)

ZHANG:

The felons are here, Your Honour.

BAO:

Remove their cangues, Zhang Qian, and dismiss the runner.
(The cangues are removed.)

LITTLE WANG:

Let's go home now, mother.

BAO:

Where do you think you are going? This is not your county office. Zhang Qian, I take it these three young men are the murderers, but who is the old woman? Is she a witness or some relation? Speak up, woman. Are these two young men related to you?

WIFE:

They are my sons.

BAO:

    And the boy?

WIFE:

    He is my youngest.

BAO:

    So this is the way you taught your sons! In ancient times the mother of Mencius moved house in order to find good neighbours for her son. The mother of Tao made him cut his hair before seeing guests, and the mother of Chen taught her son until he wore the official purple and golden belt. But you, a village woman, have taught your sons to kill a noble. Confess the truth now!

WIFE:

> *I am wretched to think my sons have broken the law,*
> *But that scoundrel's crime was more than they could bear,*
> *And they should be forgiven for killing him.*
> *We are poor, humble folk, Your Honour must protect us!*
> *These three lads are all diligent students,*
> *Whose conduct has always been guided by the classics—*
> *How could they have plotted to kill him?*
> *Tortured and beaten, they cannot put their case,*
> *But how could three of them have made this plot?*

BAO:

    You will not confess without a beating. Zhang Qian, give them a good beating.

WIFE *(weeping)*:

> My sons have broken the law:
> Was it for this they studied the Confucian classics?
> The poor lads are beaten black and blue,
> Their flesh is torn, their bones splintered—

> *Much worse than self-inflicted pain during study[20]*
> *Brought up by loving parents,*
> *They never knew such agony before.*

BAO:

One of these three youths must be the ringleader. Which of you was responsible for that man's death?

BIG WANG:

My mother and brothers had nothing to do with this. I killed him.

MIDDLE WANG:

Your Honour, my mother and brothers had nothing to do with this. I killed him.

LITTLE WANG:

Your Honour, my mother and brothers had nothing to do with this, and neither had I.

WIFE:

My three sons had nothing to do with this. When that noble, Ge Biao, beat my husband to death, I could not choke back my anger. So I fought with him and killed him. It was my doing.

BAO:

Nonsense! You all admit to murder—this is a plot. We must find the true murderer to make him pay with his life. Zhang Qian, give them another beating.

WIFE:

> *No one will speak up to save them;*
> *I have to look on, helpless.*
> Make a clean breast of things, sons!
> I will plead again with the prefect.

---

[20] Diligent scholars in the old days sometimes fastened their hair to a beam or pricked their legs to keep themselves awake

That bully murdered my husband,
Yet Your Honour had me arrested
By runners as fierce as tigers and wolves.
Do not be angry. Your Honour!
You have instruments of torture, hammer and screws.
And you question these lads again and again,
Beating them till the blood streams from their wounds.
My eldest boy cries out at this injustice,
But Your Honour turns a deaf ear;
My second is suffering the torments of hell—
How can he bear such torture?
My third is beaten even more cruelly,
And the sight makes my heart bleed.
We gaze at each other, weeping.
You are killing them, Your Honour!
Their father thought his sons would do well;
Now we cannot put our case, we can only sigh;
My heart is broken, my tears stream down like rain.

BAO:

Let me read the charge. *(He looks at it.)* What a fool the magistrate of Zhongmou County must be! This charge says that Big Wang, Middle Wang and Little Wang beat to death the noble Ge Biao. Hasn't he got a proper secretary? These three lads must have names, or at least nicknames. What is your eldest son's name, woman?

WIFE:

Gold.

BAO:

And your second son's?

WIFE:

Iron.

BAO:

And the third?

116

WIFE:
>Stone.

LITTLE WANG:
>Broke.

BAO:
>What do you mean, broke?

LITTLE WANG:
>Stony broke.

BAO:
>Stop cracking jokes. This is a murder case. Why should common citizens choose such unusual names? Did Gold Wang kill this man?

WIFE:
>*Gold is not hard to refine.*

BAO:
>Did Stone Wang kill this man?

WIFE:
>*Stone is strong and true.*

BAO:
>Did Iron Wang kill this man?

WIFE:
>*Even iron would melt in the furnace of the law.*

BAO:
>Have these stubborn scoundrels beaten!

WIFE:
>*They are not being stubborn:*
>*They are unjustly accused!*

BAO:

You know the proverb: A murderer must pay with his life, a debtor must pay his debt. Have the eldest taken out and executed, Zhang Qian.

WIFE:

I look on and cannot save him—
He is being dragged down the steps!
I am at my wit's end!
What a fool this prefect is!

BAO:

What did that woman say just now when I ordered her eldest son to be executed?

ZHANG:

She clutched the cangue and called Your Honour a fool.

BAO:

So she called me a fool, did she? Bring her over here.
(She kneels before the prefect)

BAO:

I decreed that your eldest son should pay with his life. Why did you call me a fool?

WIFE:

How dare I call Your Honour such a name? But this boy is a good son. If you kill him, who will support me?

BAO:

Since his mother says the eldest is a good son, and the neighbours will vouch for him, I must be wrong. Let the eldest live to support her. Zhang Qian, take the second son to be executed.

WIFE:

I cannot bear to give up Gold,
Yet Iron's death would also break my heart.
If we must pay with a life,
Let my boys be spared

And let me die in their place.
This cruel prefect will not listen to reason,
So I cling to the cangue and cry that injustice is done!
What a fool this prefect is!

BAO:

What did that woman call out this time?

ZHANG:

Your Honour, she called you a fool again.

BAO:

Bring her over here.
(She kneels before the prefect)

BAO:

See here, woman, I have just sentenced your second son instead. Why did you call me a fool again?

WIFE:

How dare I call Your Honour such a name? But my second son has a good head for business. If you kill him, who will support me?

BAO:

When I sentence your eldest to death, you say he is a good son. When I sentence your second to death, you say he has a good head for business. Who is to pay for the crime then?
(Little Wang puts on a cangue himself)

BAO:

What is that boy doing?

LITTLE WANG:

Since my eldest brother is not to die, nor my second brother either, it looks as if it will be me. So I may as well make a noble gesture.

BAO:

All right. Zhang Qian, take the youngest to be executed.
(Little Wang is pushed away)

BAO:

Well, woman, do you agree to let your youngest pay for the crime?

WIFE:

Yes. The proverb says: When there are three partners, the youngest shoulders the hardships. He is the one who should pay.

BAO:

Am I a fool or not?

WIFE:

Your Honour is not.

BAO:

Wait! Zhang Qian, bring him back. I was nearly taken in by this woman. I see now that this is a case of different treatment for one's own children and those adopted. These two older lads must be your own sons, while the youngest is adopted. As you have no fondness for him, you want him to pay for the crime. Speak up, woman. If you tell the truth, I shall take steps accordingly. If you lie, I shall not spare you.

WIFE:

All three are my sons. What do you want me to confess?

BAO:

Since she won't tell the truth, Zhang Qian, beat them!

WIFE:

Sons, I shall have to tell the truth. Don't hold it against me.

BAO:

Is the eldest boy your own?

WIFE:

He is not my son, but I nurse him.

BAO:

How about the second?

WIFE:

I tended him as a child.

BAO:

And the youngest?

WIFE *(weeping):*

He is my own. The others are adopted.

BAO:

Now look here, woman, aren't you making a mistake? Wouldn't it be better to let one of the adopted sons pay for this crime, and keep your own child to support you?

WIFE:

That would not be right, Your Honour. If I let the first wife's son die, it would look as if I were a heartless stepmother. If I took advantage of these boys, I should blush to remember those virtuous mothers of old.

BAO:

Well, woman, to be fair to them, you must tell the truth. Who killed that man?

WIFE:

How can I make reply?
I will not answer this question.
Their flesh is in shreds,
They stream with blood,
This is a living hell!
All my three boys may be killed,
For officials are all related,
And the prefect takes the side of the dead noble.
(She weeps)
Now if my eldest son dies for this crime,
My second forfeits his life as well,

And my third becomes a shade too,
I shall be left alone, a poor old woman.
Gold is good to his mother,
Iron, if set free, will support the family:
So say no more, Stony,
It is right you should pay with your life;
The third of three partners is always the one to suffer,
And now the runners are shouting again.

BAO:

Hearing this woman, I realize the truth of the saying: A clever merchant will appear to have no goods, and a worthy gentleman will look like a fool. I see what fine people this mother and her sons are—they stand comparison with the men of old. As I was dozing just now, I dreamed that a butterfly caught in a spider's web was rescued by a big butterfly. When this had happened twice, another small butterfly was caught, but instead of saving it the large one flew away. As my heart was touched, I saved the little creature myself. In fact, Heaven was forewarning me of this case so that I might save the boy's life.

I weighed the case according to the law,
But this suit is most involved.
The murder of a noble cannot be pardoned,
Nor the culprit go unpunished.
First I sentenced the eldest lad to death,
But she said he was a good son;
When I sentenced the second,
She said he must support her;
When I sentenced the third,
She was pleased and let him go.
She showed most kindness to the adopted sons,
And hardened her heart against her own flesh and blood.
Such virtuous conduct is most praiseworthy,
Such a good mother deserves to be rewarded.
This flashed into my mind
Because Heaven had given me warning
Through the dream of three butterflies caught in a web.

That was precisely the case of this mother and sons:
Three times she spoke, and abandoned her own child,
Exactly as I saw in my dream at noon. Zhang Qian, take all three of them to the condemned cell.

WIFE *(trying desperately to stop them):*

They are dragging and pushing them off;
I seize the cangue and cry out against such injustice!
They are going, never to return.
I am distracted. What if I die with them?
Yes, best to share their death;
Let me catch hold of their clothes. (Zhang Qian pushes her away and takes the three sons off.)

WIFE:

This prefect has a reputation for justice,
But today he passed wrong judgement.
He sits in the court with his insignia of office,
And draws a high salary—but all for what?
My sons are unjustly condemned and thrown into gaol.
I am desperate—I must act.
Shall I appeal to the provincial governor,
Beat the court drum in the capital,
Or call aloud before the imperial carriage?
No, who would pay any heed to a foolish woman?
To die would be better than to live on alone
With no one to support me,
Weeping and wretched to the end of my days. (Exit.)

BAO:

Come here, Zhang Qian! What do you think of all this?

ZHANG:

Are you sure you are right, Your Honour?

BAO:

Do you question my orders, you rascal?
Well I serve my sagacious sovereign,

My fame will endure through the ages;
Unless I pass just sentence on this case,
How can I be the prefect of Kaifeng? (Exeunt.)

ACT III

(Enter Zhang Qian.)

ZHANG:

A pitiless club in my hands,
Tear-stained money in my pockets;
A tiger or wolf by day,
At night I sleep beside corpses. I am Zhang Qian. Now the three Wang brothers are in the condemned cell. Let me have them in. *(Enter Big and Middle Wang.)*

BOTH:

Have pity on us, brother!

ZHANG:

Turn those cangues round, and let me give you three strokes apiece. *(He beats them)* Where is the third? *(Enter Little Wang.)*

LITTLE WANG:

Here I am.
(Enter Li Wan)

ZHANG:

Li Wan, bring that bed over and pass me the rope. Let's truss them up tight. *(He pulls the rope and the boys groan)* Now, Li Wan, go and have your meal while I look after them. I hope the gaoler doesn't turn up. *(Exit Li Wan. Enter Wang's Wife.)*

WIFE:

All my three sons are in the condemned cell. I have been begging and got some scraps of food for them.
Coming from the alms-house to the prison,
Not daring to lose a second,
I have begged from door to door
And got some left-overs—noodles and dumplings.
My sons were going to pass the examination,
Sit in courtrooms and draw high pay;

But instead they got into this trouble!
They have done nothing wrong,
We skimped and scraped,
And slept on the bare ground—
No one ever put up with such poverty.
As the proverb says: Good sons
Are better than riches and rank.
For this I put up with much.
(She reaches the gaol gate)
Here I am. I'll pull the bell.

ZHANG:

I'm afraid the gaoler is here. Let me open the gate and see who it is.

WIFE:

It is me.

ZHANG *(striking her):*

Is this your home, old crone? What are you doing here?

WIFE:

I've brought some food for my three sons.

ZHANG:

They have paid me nothing for the lamp oil and this thankless job. I have to live on these gaol-birds, so give me what money you have.

WIFE:

Have a heart, brother! My old man was beaten to death and my three sons are here in gaol. I can barely keep going myself, and have simply begged some scraps for my hungry children. Don't be hard on us!
Beggars' scraps heated up again,
Rags I have mended;
Take this tattered coat, brother,
And this old sleeve as a tip.

ZHANG:

    I don't want them.

WIFE:

    Please keep an eye on these wretches;
    Have pity on them, brother.

ZHANG:

    Sentence has already been passed. I can't help them now.

WIFE:

    We are one loving family,
    My heart bleeds for these boys,
    My tears rain down.
    It is unjust to accuse them of a crime;
    I call on Heaven, and beg you to have pity.
    There they lie, rolling their eyes,
    Trembling in every limb.
    I have cried myself hoarse to save them,
    And despair has bent me double.

ZHANG:

    All right. Come in. Let me close the gate.

WIFE *(entering the gaol*

    ): My poor children!
    (The three boys weep)

BIG WANG:

    Mother, what are you doing here?

WIFE:

    I've brought you food. *(She turns to Zhang)* Could you set them free, brother, to eat?

ZHANG:

    Haven't you got hands, woman? Feed them yourself.

WIFE *(feeding her two elder sons):*

I stumble forward to feed my boys. Spoon after spoon I satisfy their hunger, Drop after drop I quench their thirst.

LITTLE WANG:

Give me a little, mother.

WIFE:

Here's a mouthful for you, boy.
(She puts the food on the ground)
Here is some bread for you, Gold. Don't let Stony see it. Here is some bread for you, Iron. Don't let Stony see it.
Beggars' leavings, no rich fare,
No scholars' feast in the imperial hall.
You were hauled here from the county court in cangues,
Not walking as candidates to the golden palace.
Ah, this will be the death of me!
But it is useless to murmur against the gaol.
I am going, Gold. Have you anything to say?

BIG WANG:

There is a volume of the *Four Books* at home, mother. Sell it to buy paper money for father's sacrifice.

WIFE:

Have you anything to say, Iron?

MIDDLE WANG:

I have a volume of Mencius, mother. Sell it to pay for father's sacrifice.

LITTLE WANG *(weeping):*

I have nothing. Let me stroke your head a moment. *(Their mother goes out.)*

ZHANG:

Hey, woman! Do you want some good news?

WIFE:

Indeed I do.

ZHANG *(entering the gaol):*

Where is the eldest son?

BIG WANG:

Here.

ZHANG:

You can go.
(Big Wang leaves the gaol!)
Hey, woman, since this eldest boy is a good son, you can take him back to look after you. Are you glad to see him?

WIFE:

Indeed I am!

ZHANG:

I'll give you some more good news. *(He enters the gaol again!)* Where is the second son?

MIDDLE WANG:

Here.

ZHANG:

Get up, you can go too. *(He lets Middle Wang out.)* Hey, woman! As your second boy has a good head for business, you can take him back to support you.

WIFE:

How about my youngest?

ZHANG:

He will be hanged till he is dead, to pay for the death of Ge Biao. Come first thing tomorrow to pick up his corpse outside the wall.

WIFE:

The two elder boys are free,
But the third is a prisoner still.
After all that I went through,

Carrying and nursing him!
But if I let his elder brothers be killed,
They will call me a heartless stepmother.
This is unjust—you are bearing the brunt for others;
Still, a life must pay for a life,
So die content!
(She looks back at Little Wang.)
If I keep turning back again and again,
They will say I am faint-hearted.

BIG and MIDDLE WANG:

Mother, how can we leave our brother to die?

WIFE:

Come home with me, children. Don't grieve for him.
Your unhappy younger brother will be killed
And go to the nether regions.
(She gazes at Little Wang and weeps.)
I turn back and shed tears.
(The two brothers weep.) All right, let us go.
He will die content.
Poor child, so young in years,
We shall never meet again.
I cannot let the sons of others be killed,
Or later generations will reproach me.
I stamp my foot in despair three dozen times.
Tomorrow he will lie dead in the market-place;
I shall never see Stony again.
Before I have burned the paper money for my husband,
My child is found guilty too.
When will son and father meet?
In dreams alone
Shall I see my son again.
(She goes out, followed by Big Wang and Middle Wang.)

LITTLE WANG:

Where are my brothers?

ZHANG:

By His Honour's orders, your two brothers have been pardoned and sent home to support your mother. You alone will pay for Ge Biao's death.

LITTLE WANG:

So my two brothers are spared, and I must pay with my life. Put the two other cangues on me then. Though I alone am to die, the three of us are one. How shall I die tomorrow, brother?

ZHANG:

You will be hanged till you are dead, then thrown over this thirty-foot wall.

LITTLE WANG:

Be careful when you throw me, brother. I have a boil on my belly.

ZHANG:

You'll be dead by then.

LITTLE WANG:

A bellyful of learning....

ZHANG:

So you still want to sing, eh?

LITTLE WANG:

Yes, my last song.... *is no use to me at all.*
I studied the Book of Rites, *the* Book of Change,
But death has caught up with me.
My ambition was to be a high official,
But now all fame and wealth have passed me by.
This prefect is an irresponsible judge,
My father was a fool to make me study,
And I am no brilliant scholar after all,
To get myself beaten with a bastinado.
The prefect is a foolish bureaucrat,

The clerks pretend to know nothing,
And the runners ranged in the court
Are a worthless bunch of fellows.
By being thrown over the wall
I shall win renown throughout the empire,
And a curse on you, Zhang Qian!
(He goes out, followed by Zhang Qian.)

ACT IV

(Little Wang carries in Donkey Zhao's corpse, and crouches on the ground. Enter Big Wang and Middle Wang)

BIG and MIDDLE WANG:

We have come with our mother to look for Stony's body. This way, mother! *(Enter Wang's Wife)*

WIFE:

We hear that Little Wang has been hanged, so his two brothers have gone to fetch the corpse. I have begged some cash to buy sacrificial paper money. I have also brought some firewood to burn and bury his body.

> *Before dawn I slipped out of the city,*
> *Fearful lest folk should find out*
> *And make trouble for me.*
> *I have bought some paper with money I begged,*
> *And picked up a few sticks of firewood.*
> *To think that my son should die like this—*
> *Without a mat to cover him or a coffin.*
> *(She weeps)*
> *Ah, my son, unjustly killed,*
> *You will meet your father at the dividing line,*
> *Where you must work together*
> *To push the wicked murderer down to hell!*
> *The dark sky is turning white,*
> *All is quiet in this lonely stretch of country,*
> *At a distance some men are approaching,*
> *And watching their shadowy forms, I tremble with fear.*
> *(Big Wang and Middle Wang approach, carrying a corpse)*

BOTH:

Where are you, mother? Here is our brother's body.

WIFE *(glancing at it and weeping)*:

> *I look hastily at the body,*
> *A corpse bespattered with blood!*

> *With haste I undo the rope*
> *And swiftly loosen the straps.*
> *Come quickly and help me!*
> *Take his head, holding the chin,*
> *While from high ground I call back his spirit.* Ah, my child!
> *In your haste you have lost your shoes;*
> *I call, but you do not answer.*
> *I weep and mourn in vain.*
> Ah, Stony, my son!
> *I call you with all the strength in my old body,*
> *Calling your pet name clearly—*
> *Where is my good son Stony?*
> *Why have you left your mother?*
> *In vain I beat the ground,*
> *In vain I sob and stamp;*
> *I cannot call back your spirit;*
> *This will drive me out of my mind.* Stony, child!

LITTLE WANG *(standing up):*

> Here I am!

WIFE:

> *What is that answering voice?*
> *Where could it come from?*
> *Can it be some mountain goblin?*

LITTLE WANG:

> I am here, mother.

WIFE:

> A ghost! A ghost!

LITTLE WANG:

> Don't be afraid, mother. I am your son Stony.

WIFE:

> *He follows me as I run,*
> *I am at my wit's end in terror.*
> *Trembling, I bow before my dead son—*

I shall make good sacrifice to you.

LITTLE WANG:

Mother, I am flesh and blood.

WIFE:

If you are not a ghost,
Tell me quickly
How you escaped.

LITTLE WANG:

His Honour hanged that horse thief, Donkey Zhao, and told me to carry his corpse out. Me he spared.

WIFE:

So all our troubles are over!
My sorrow ended, I laugh.
I thought you were gone
Like a pebble in the ocean.
But my elder sons deserve a scolding.
What were you about?
Don't grumble if I blame you.
How could you be so offhand as to carry another's corpse here?
You should have kept your eyes open,
Instead of bringing me a stranger's corpse.
Yet what happiness this is,
What a miracle wrought by fairies!
You, the youngest, were sentenced to death—
How was it you were spared?

LITTLE WANG:

I knew I should be all right.

WIFE:

So it is true that honesty prevails!
Let us bury this corpse
Which was carried here by mistake. (Enter the prefect!)

BAO:

What! Are you committing another murder? *(Wang's Wife and her sons are frightened.)*

BAO:

Don't be alarmed. That is the corpse of the horse thief, Donkey Zhao. He has paid in your place for the death of Ge Biao. Now listen to His Majesty's orders:
You are the sovereign's good subjects,
Worthy to serve the state as officers.
The eldest son shall have a post at court,
The second son shall be a high official,
The third shall be Magistrate of Zhongmou County,
And their mother shall be a lady;
For the court sets store by virtuous wives and mothers,
And values those who are good sons to their parents.
So our sage emperor rewards you all.
Face the capital and thank His Majesty!

ALL:

Long live the emperor!

WIFE:

An amnesty has come down from highest Heaven,
And we no longer complain about the verdict,
But face the capital and bow our thanks,
Hoping our emperor will live for ever.
Like a withered tree which blooms again,
After beating and imprisonment
Our sadness has turned to joy,
Our debt of sorrow is paid,
We have left the castle of darkness.
May Your Honour rise to be chief minister,
With fresh promotion each day.
Now the mother has a lady's rank,
And her son is made Magistrate of Zhongmou.
So mother and son will live together in peace,

Free from all calamities, great and small.
May our gracious sovereign reign on his throne for ever!
(THE END)

RESCUED BY A COQUETTE

CHARACTERS
ZHOU SHE, *a profligate*
MISTRESS SONG, *a widow*
SONG YINZHANG, *her daughter, a singsong girl*
AN XIUSHI, *a scholar*
ZHAO PANER, *a singsong girl*
WAITER
ZHANG, *an errand boy*
LI GONGBI, *Prefect of Zhengzhou*
ATTENDANTS

ACT I

(Enter Zhou She.)

ZHOU:

Thirty years I've been a glutton,
Twenty years I've been lucky with girls.
I never know the price of rice or firewood,
For all my money goes on wine and women. I am Zhou She, son of a sub-prefect and a native of Zhengzhou. Since boyhood I've haunted bawdy-houses. Now here in Bianliang is a singsong girl called Song Yinzhang. We want to marry each other, but her mother won't give her consent. I'm just back from a business trip. Today is a lucky day, so I'm going to their house to say "How do you do?" to her mother and propose this match. Here I go. *(Enter Mistress Song and her daughter.)*

MRS. SONG:

A flower may blossom again, But youth never returns. I am a native of Bianliang. My family name is Li, but I married a man named Song. My husband died early and I have only this daughter Yinzhang. She's clever at jokes and puns and a good hand at quips and pranks. Zhou She of Zhengzhou has been her admirer for several years, and they want to marry each other; but I keep putting it off, afraid she might suffer for it later.

YINZHANG:

Don't worry about that, mother. I've set my heart on having him.

MRS. SONG:

Have it your own way then. *(Enter Zhou She.)*

ZHOU:

Here comes Zhou She. This is their house. I'll go in. *(He greets Yinzhang.)*

YINZHANG:

So it's you, Zhou She.

ZHOU:

    I have come about our marriage. What does your mother say?

YINZHANG:

    Mother is willing.

ZHOU:

    Then let me speak to her. *(He greets Mistress Song.)* I have come about this marriage, ma'am.

MRS. SONG:

    Today is a lucky day: I give my consent. But mind you don't ill-treat my child.

ZHOU:

    How dare I ill-treat her? Invite all our friends, ma'am, and I'll make myself ready and come.

MRS. SONG:

    Keep an eye on the house, child, while I go to invite my old friends. *(Exeunt.)*

YINZHANG:

    Mother has gone. Let me see who is coming now. *(Exit.) (Enter the scholar An Xiushi.)*

AN:

    Qu Yuan drowned himself, leaving eternal sorrow;
All his life, poor Yan Hui remained steadfast in his aim.
    I am An Xiushi, a native of Loyang. I have always enjoyed women and wine. Here in Bianliang is a singsong girl called Song Yinzhang, who is my sweetheart. She promised to marry me, but now she is marrying Zhou She. She has a sworn sister, Zhao Paner. And I'm on my way to ask Paner for help. Here I am. Are you at home, sister? *(Enter Paner.)*

142

PANER:

I am Zhao Paner. I was going to do some needlework, but I hear someone calling. Let me open the door and see who it is. *(She greets An.)* I was wondering who it was. So it's my sister's betrothed. Where have you come from?

AN:

I have come to ask you a favour. Your sister Yinzhang promised to marry me, but now she's agreed to marry Zhou She instead. I want you to speak to her!

PANER:

Yes, she gave you her promise, didn't she? But now she wants to marry someone else. Really, getting married is a difficult business!

> *Though we singsong girls make money by pleasing men,*
> *We can find no devoted admirers in the end.*
> *No match should be made by force,*
> *Or hurried through before the time is ripe.*
> *If two people marry as soon as they fall in love,*
> *A day will come when they repent their rashness.*
> *The future is dark as the never-fathomed ocean;*
> *Men's hearts are a riddle which*
> *Heaven alone can make out.*
> *To marry, you need a couple,*
> *And each one hopes to find a perfect mate;*
> *We make our choice a hundred, thousand times,*
> *Seeking an honest man—but can we find one?*
> *Seeking a clever fellow—but will he prove constant?*
> *As it is, we are thrown away on curs and swine;*
> *We fall suddenly to the ground,*
> *And wake to find we have only ourselves to blame.*
> *I have known young brides in my time,*
> *But a few days of harsh treatment*
> *Make haggard ghosts of them;*
> *Yet they cannot express their despair*
> *Or tell their sorrow.*

I have seen ambitious beauties fare like that.
I would rather sleep alone the whole of my life!

Brother, I am going to get married myself, so I know what these would-be brides are like.

AN:

What are they like?

PANER:

They want to be honest and learn the wifely virtues,
But all singsong girls are considered light and giddy:
This is really the lowest trade;
Though I live in luxury, what good does it do me?
We live by cheating others,
But men torment us too,
In wicked, unnatural ways.
Each mother's son is a scoundrel.

If a fellow comes two or three times and we don't ask him for money, the wretch says we have designs on him.

Yet we won't see through him,
But fall in love with him.
Some women envy singsong girls,
Some envy concubines;
But the girl who wants to marry
Is out for wealth and a good reputation,
While the girl who simply pretends to want to marry
Is hoping to marry money.
Though the girl who marries is bound to be deceived,
Others still tread in her steps,
Instead of learning a lesson from her despair.

Take a seat, brother, while I go to persuade her. Don't be too pleased if she takes my advice, and don't be too sad if she doesn't.

AN:

I won't stay, but go home to wait for your news. Please do your best for me, sister! *(Exit.) (.Enter Yinzhang.)*

PANER *(meeting Yinzhang):*

> That's a stag with sharp antlers.
> Whom are you going to call on, sister?

YINZHANG:

> I'm not calling on anyone. I'm getting married.

PANER:

> I've just come to propose a match to you.

YINZHANG:

> With whom?

PANER:

> The scholar An.

YINZHANG *(crossly):*

> If I marry him, we'll have to go begging together.

PANER:

> Well, whom do you mean to marry?

YINZHANG:

> I'm going to marry Zhou She.

PANER:

> Aren't you too young to marry?

YINZHANG:

> Why? Singsong girl today, singsong girl tomorrow: this is a wretched life. If I marry some Zhang or Li and become a respectable woman, I can hold my head up even when I'm a ghost.

PANER:

> *You had better think again!*
> *You are still quite young;*
> *Why not wait until I find you a good husband*
> *With whom you can live in comfort all your life?*
> *Your elder sister is telling you the truth:*

You won't be able to stand a husband long.

Some good husbands make good lovers too, sister. But good lovers may not make good husbands.

YINZHANG:

What do you mean?

PANER:

Though some husbands make poor lovers,
The lovers are false, while the husbands at least are honest!

YINZHANG:

But Zhou She looks so handsome in his fine clothes!

PANER:

Though he decks himself out in fine feathers,
What does he know of how to treat a wife?
Why do you want to marry him, sister?

YINZHANG:

Because he's so good to me.

PANER:

In what way is he good to you?

YINZHANG:

He cares for me all the year round. In summer, when I take a nap he fans me. In winter, he warms the quilt for me. When I dress to go out, he helps me straighten my clothes. When I put on my trinkets, he helps me pin them on. It's because he's so good to me that I want to marry him.

PANER:

So that's the reason!
I can hardly keep from laughing!
In summer, you say, he fans you to sleep
Warms your padded clothes
And your quilt at the brazier in winter.

*At table he takes his spoon
To remove the skin and gristle from your meat;
And when you go out he straightens the folds of your dress,
Pins on your trinkets and places the combs in your hair.
All this is done to deceive you;
Yet you won't see through him, but fall in love with him!
You say your lover is good to you;
But once you marry him and go to his house
Within a few months he will cast you off,
And you will be quite helpless.
He'll kick you and punch you until you burst into tears;
But by then, with the boat in mid-stream,
It will be too late for you to stop the leak,
And whom will you have to blame?
So look before you leap!
I know, if I can't convince you,
That some fine day I shall have to rescue you!*
Don't come running to me when he starts ill-treating you!

YINZHANG:

Even if I'm condemned to death, I shan't ask for your help!
(Enter Zhou She with porters.)

ZHOU:

Display the presents, men.

PANER:

So Zhou She is coming. If he says nothing, well and good. If he speaks, I shall give him a tongue-lashing!

ZHOU:

Is that Sister Zhao?

PANER:

It is.

ZHOU:

Won't you have some tea and food with us?

PANER:

Are you asking me home to a meal? You serve hungry guests from an empty pan—what food can I expect from you?

ZHOU:

I want you to act as voucher.

PANER:

As voucher for whom?

ZHOU:

For Yinzhang here.

PANER:

So you want me to vouch for her? You want me to vouch that she'll do all a housewife's work—sew, cook, embroider, make clothes and bear you children?

ZHOU:

Oh, what a tongue you have! Well, since I've succeeded already, I can do without your help.

PANER:

I'll be going then. *(She walks out.)*
(Enter An.)

AN:

Well, sister, how did your talk with Yinzhang go?

PANER:

It made no impression at all.

AN:

In that case, I'd better go to the capital to sit for the examination.

PANER:

Don't go yet. I need you here.

AN:

    Whatever you say. I'll stay on in the inn, and see what you can do for me. *(Exit.)*

PANER:

> *She's a fox-fairy, witch, a vampire who sucks men's blood,*
> *With no human legs in her trousers!*
> *Though you spit out blood for her, ah,*
> *She thinks nothing of it!*
> *You must sow no more wild oats,*
> *For it's easy to make her jealous,*
> *But must stick to her side to please her.*
> Look out, An Xiushi, I warn you!
> *You have made ready wedding robes and a gold tiara.*
> *You think you have won a wife.*
> *But she's marrying another for his money! (Exit.)*

ZHOU:

    When you've said goodbye to your mother, my dear, get in the sedan-chair and we'll set off to Zhengzhou. *(Exeunt.)*

ACT II

(Enter Zhou She.)

ZHOU:

I am Zhou She. After riding horses all my life, I've ended up on a donkey. I practically wore out my tongue to get this woman. On a lucky day I managed at last to mount her in a sedan and ride out of Bianliang with her towards Zhengzhou. I let her travel by chair in front so that people wouldn't laugh at me for marrying a singsong girl. But when I saw the chair tossing up and down, I rode across to beat the bearers. "How dare you make fun of me like this?" I asked. And I raised my whip to beat them. "Just carry the chair," I said. "Why toss it up and down?" "It's not us," said the bearers. "It's the lady inside." When I lifted the curtain o with my whip, what do you think I saw? She had stripped herself naked and was turning somersaults! When we got home I told her to sew me a quilt; but when I went in, there was the quilt standing up as high as the bedposts. "Yinzhang! Where are you?" I shouted. "I'm in here, Zhou She!" she called from inside the quilt. "What are you doing in there?" "When I put in the cotton, I sewed myself in by mistake." I took up a stick to beat her. "You can beat me, Zhou She," she said. "But mind you don't beat our neighbour, Mistress Wang." "A fine thing!" said I. "So you've sewn up the neighbour too!" When the belt on my coat got loose, I told her to sew it on. "I've done it," she said. "Where is it?" I asked. "I've sewn it strongly," she answered. I looked all round, but couldn't find it. Where could it be? When I picked up a mirror to look at myself, I found it sewn on my shoulder. That's the way you behave, you slut. I may beat you or kill you, but I won't sell you or let you go. I'm going out now for a drink. When I come back, I'll give you a proper hiding. *(Exit.) (Enter Yinzhang.)*

YINZHANG:

Ignore good advice, and you're bound to get into trouble! When Paner warned me against him, I wouldn't listen to her. But the moment I crossed his threshold he gave me fifty strokes to be going on with. There's a pedlar in this neighbourhood named

Wang, who is going to Bianliang on business. I'll ask him to take a note to my mother, so that she and Paner can rescue me. If they don't come soon, they'll find me dead. Heaven knows, I'm likely to be beaten to death! *(Exit.)*

(Enter Mistress Song, crying.)

MRS. SONG:

My heart is full of grief,
But I am silent.

I'm the mother of Yinzhang who married Zhou She. Yesterday Pedlar Wang brought me a letter from her in which she said: "The moment I crossed Zhou's threshold he gave me fifty strokes to be going on with; since when he's been beating and cursing me day and night. Please ask Paner to come at once to save me." I'm taking this letter now to show Paner, to ask her how we can rescue my unfortunate daughter. Ah, child, you'll be the death of your poor mother! *(Exit) (Enter Paner)*

PANER:

I am Zhao Paner. When shall I be able to leave this wretched profession, I wonder? I want to find a husband too, and now is a good time.

I'm longing to marry and settle down,
But I've never heard of a man
Willing to clear a singsong girl's debts and redeem her.
All they do is to fawn on the rich in their splendid mansions,
Not caring if they ruin the courtesans' quarters,
Floundering like fish escaping from a net,
Or flapping, if something goes wrong, like wounded pigeons.
We girls are roadside willows,
And good families will not take in courtesans;
Our lovers seem sincere in the beginning,
But as they grow old they forget their former sweethearts.
They take pleasure for a time,
Then swiftly go their way,

heaving us all too quickly
hike foam on the waves.
For them we offend our master and our mistress
Till we are as far apart as sun and moon,
Yet we let ourselves be taken in
By their ardent looks and ten thousand vows of love.
How soon all these are forgotten!
Let me see who is coming. *(Enter Mistress Song)*

MRS. SONG:

This is her door. Let me go in. *(Greeting her.)*
Paner, I am so worried!

PANER:

Why are you crying so bitterly, mother?

MRS. SONG:

Let me tell you. Though you warned her against him, Yinzhang would marry Zhou She; but the moment she crossed his threshold he gave her fifty strokes to be going on with. And now he is beating her so cruelly he'll soon kill her. What shall I do, Paner?

PANER:

Oh, Yinzhang, have you been beaten?
I remember how you arranged your marriage in secret,
And today you are enemies:
My warnings have come true!
You left here only last autumn,
Thinking you had found a good husband,
Hoping his love for you would last for ever,
Clinging fondly to his hand;
But as soon as you crossed his threshold it was over!
He is beating you every day, and you want to escape;
If I do not save your life,
I shall be ashamed when I think of our former friendship.
Ah, why did she marry a man like this?

MRS. SONG:

Zhou She swore he would be true, Paner.

PANER:

All of them swear they will die before they stop loving;
All of them break their word.
You were too simple, mother,
To believe a young man who was courting a girl.
Zhou She is not the only liar, mother.
All of them swear great oaths,
But like wind that brushes your ear their vows are lost.

MRS. SONG:

But tell me, Paner, how can I rescue my child?

PANER:

I have two silver ingots I've saved, mother. Let's use them to buy her back.

MRS. SONG:

He said he would beat her to death, but never sell her.
(Paner reflects, then whispers something to Mistress Song.)

PANER:

This is the only way.

MRS. SONG:

But will it work?

PANER:

Don't worry. May I see her letter?
(Mistress Song passes her the note, and Paner reads it.)

PANER:

"Yinzhang greets her sister Paner and her mother. It has happened just as you said. Because I wouldn't listen to good advice, I am having a terrible time. The moment I crossed his threshold he gave me fifty strokes to be going on with; since when he's been beating and cursing me day and night. If you come soon, you will still be able to see me; but if you don't come soon, you'll find me dead." Ah, sister! Who told you to do such a foolish thing?

We used to share all our troubles;
Now she says she may die
And become a homeless ghost,
While I do nothing to help her. Ah, sister, didn't you say, "What's the good of being a singsong girl all my life? If I marry some Zhang or Li—
And become a respectable woman,
I can hold my head up
Even when I'm a ghost."
Mother, has the messenger left?

MRS. SONG:

Not yet.

PANER:

I'll write a letter to her. *(She writes.)*
I am writing this letter myself
To bid her keep my plan secret,
And to send my greetings to the rash, foolish creature—
Poor girl, she must be aching all over now!
Now the letter is written. When I go there,
I shall dress my hair again,
And wear rich embroidery.
That fellow beats her all day long,
Under his savage rods her red blood flows;
And he treats her like a criminal.
But I shall show him my figure,
And wear emerald leaves on my forehead,
With pearls and a phoenix design.
I shall be beautifully turned out,
And with a powdered face I'll rescue her I
I've made up my mind, and mean to go through with it;
He can curse me as much as he likes when it is done!
This is no idle boast:
I shan't let the scoundrel slip through my delicate fingers!

Don't you worry, mother.

MRS. SONG:

Be careful, Paner, when you get there. Ah, child, you are worrying me to death!

PANER:

Set your heart at rest, mother,
And smooth that wrinkled forehead;
I promise to bring her home to you safe and sound.
That dangler after women
Is like a dog or donkey;
I know he'll be up to all his tricks to please me.

When I reach Zhengzhou, I shall speak to him. If he's willing to divorce her, well and good. If not, I'll pinch him and stroke him, hug him and cuddle him, till he's completely distracted. I'll put sugar under his nose that he can't lick and can't eat until he divorces Yinzhang. But when she has her divorce paper and leaves him, I'll walk out on him too!

I'll charm him into losing both of us! (Exeunt.)

ACT III

(Enter Zhou She and a Waiter)

ZHOU:

If all that happens is fated,
Why should men toil and moil?

It wasn't to make money that I let you open this inn, waiter. But if any attractive girls come here, call me over at once.

WAITER:

All right. But how am I to find you?

ZHOU:

Look for me in the courtesans' quarters.

WAITER:

And if I can't find you there?

ZHOU:

Then look for me in the gambling dens.

WAITER:

And if I can't find you there?

ZHOU:

Then look for me in gaol. *(Exit.)*
(Enter Zhang, the errand boy, carrying cases.)

ZHANG:

Nailed boots and umbrella:
My job is to deliver billets-doux.

I'm Zhang the errand boy. My job is to run errands for the singsong girls. I deliver their chits and bring back messages for them. Now Zhao Paner wants me to rope two chests of clothes and bedding to take to Zhengzhou. They're all ready, sister. Please mount your horse. *(Enter Paner.)*

PANER:

    Boy, am I well enough tricked out to make that fellow fall for me? *(Zhang falls to the ground.)*

PANER:

    What are you doing?

ZHANG:

    Don't talk about *him* falling for you. I've just fallen badly myself.

PANER:

> *Yinzhang is in such a tight corner,*
> *She doesn't know what to do.*
> *The silly child acted so rashly*
> *That I shall have to use all my charms to save her.*
> *I must wheedle that donkey and coax him,*
> *Till he leaves his stable to trot after me,*
> *While I act as if there's no better man in the world.*
> *This may sound easy, but it takes an effort,*
> *And several times I've felt like giving up;*
> *But I pity her poor, helpless mother,*
> *And because I've no home of my own*
> *I can sympathize with others,*
> Just as a drinker sympathizes with drunkards.
> So I mean to spare no pains.

    Now we've arrived at Zhengzhou. Take the horse, boy. We'll rest for a while in the willow's shade.

ZHANG:

    Very good.

PANER:

    You know, boy, people from good families have good manners, and people from bad families bad manners.

ZHANG:

    What do you mean, sister?

PANER:

> *A lady is always a lady,*
> *A singsong girl is always a singsong girl.*
> *I may mince along in my husband's house,*
> But I'll find it hard to keep all the household rules.
> Young ladies simply dust their faces with powder,
> They don't plaster it on the way we do.
> Young ladies comb their hair slowly and modestly,
> They don't loosen their clothes like us, and half choke themselves.
> Young ladies know how to act in a seemly way,
> Not like us, who run wild like monkeys locked in a room.
> So in spite of my tricks and wiles,
> In spite of all my fine talk,
> I can't hide the fact that I'm a singsong girl.

ZHANG:

Here's an inn, sister. Let's put up here.

PANER:

Call the waiter. *(The Waiter greets her!)*

PANER:

Clean out a room for me, boy, and put our luggage there; then go to ask Zhou She over. Tell him I've been waiting for him a long time.

WAITER:

All right. *(He walks out)* Master Zhou, where are you? *(Enter Zhou She)*

ZHOU:

Why are you calling me, boy?

WAITER:

There's a beautiful girl in the inn, who is asking for you.

ZHOU:

Let's go! *(He greets Paner)* She certainly is a fine-looking singsong girl!

PANER:

So, Zhou She, you've come!
How clever my sister is and how lucky,
To marry the handsomest man I've ever seen,
And such a young man tool

ZHOU:

Haven't I seen you before? Was it in that inn where you were playing a harp, and I gave you a length of brown silk?

PANER:

I don't know about that.

ZHANG:

No, I never saw any brown silk.

ZHOU:

I have it! When I left Hangzhou for Shanxi and was drinking in an inn, didn't I invite you to a meal?

PANER:

No, I never saw that.
You're so forgetful you don't recognize me,
Just like the man in the story.
We met by Peach Blossom Stream,
But today, when we meet again, you pretend not to know me,
While I have been thinking so fondly of you all this time!

ZHOU:

Ah, I remember now. Aren't you Zhao Paner?

PANER:

That's right!

ZHOU:

Well, well! You were the one who tried to break up my marriage. Here, waiter! Close the gate, and beat up that boy!

ZHANG:

Don't beat me! My sister has come with silk dresses and bedding to marry you. Why should you want to beat me?

PANER:

Sit down, Zhou She, and listen to me. When you were in the southern capital, I heard everyone talk of you, but never met you. Later, after meeting you, I couldn't take a bite or sup for thinking of you. Then I heard you were going to marry Yinzhang. I wanted to marry you, Zhou She, yet you asked me to vouch for her!

As an elder sister, I had to pretend to be pleased,
Though I was jealous and wanted to break up your match;
You look intelligent, but you must be stupid,
If you think, because you're married,
I'll give you up!

I come with carriage and horses and a dowry to give you; yet for no reason at all you curse and beat us! Boy, turn the carriage round. We're going home.

ZHOU:

If I'd known you had come to marry me, of course I wouldn't have beaten your boy.

PANER:

Do you mean it? Well, if you really didn't know, don't leave this inn but stay a few days with me.

ZHOU:

I'm willing to stay a couple of years here with you, not just a few days. *(Enter Yinzbang.)*

YINZHANG:

    Zhou She hasn't been home for several days, and now I've traced him to this inn. Let me have a look. Why, there he is, sitting with Sister Zhao! You shameless lecher, you! I've followed you all the way here. Just try to come home, Zhou She! If you do, I'll take a knife and you can take a knife, and we'll fight it out between us! *(Exit.)*

ZHOU *(seizing a stick):*

    I'll deal with you presently. If not for this lady's presence, I'd beat you to death!

PANER:

> *I never forget a grudge either;*
> *But instead of losing my temper*
> *I keep my feelings to myself.*
> *Why should you beat her here?*
> *One night of love is worth a hundred of friendship,*
> *So stop your angry fuming;*
> *And if you must be rough, be rough in private.*
> *In front of me you ought to be more careful—*
> *What lover will beat a pretty girl to death?*
> *He's still glaring and brandishing his cruel stick;*
> *Other hot-tempered men don't behave like this.*

    That's a big stick you're holding. What will happen if you beat her to death?

ZHOU:

    If a husband kills his wife, he need not pay with his life.

PANER:

    If you talk like that, who will dare to marry you?
> *I pretend not to understand, and play the coquette,*
> *So that soon he'll have no home left;*
> *For with my charms I can rescue poor Yinzbang.*

    A fine friend you are, Zhou She! Sitting here, and sending for your wife to come and abuse me! Boy, turn the carriage round. We're going home.

ZHOU:

Please sit down, ma'am. I didn't know she was coming. May I die if I knew of it!

PANER:

Are you sure? That woman is no good. If you'll get rid of her at once, I'll marry you.

ZHOU:

I'll divorce her as soon as I get home. *(Aside.)* Wait a bit, though! I've scared Yinzhang by beating her every day. If I give her a divorce, she'll dash off like a streak of smoke. And then suppose Paner backs out? Won't I be losing at both ends? I mustn't do anything rash, but get Paner to promise to marry me. *(To Paner.)* Excuse me, ma'am, I'm as stupid as a donkey or a horse. If I go home today and divorce my wife, suppose you let me down, won't I be losing at both ends? Will you make an oath, ma'am?

PANER:

So you want me to make an oath? Very well, if you divorce your wife and I refuse you, may I be trampled to death by a horse in the hall, or have my legs crushed by a lampwick. See what fearful oaths I've sworn for you!

ZHOU:

Boy, bring wine!

PANER:

There's no need to buy wine. I've ten bottles in my carriage.

ZHOU:

Then I'll buy a sheep.

PANER:

There's no need. I have one cooked already.

ZHOU:

At least let me buy the red silk.

PANER:
There's no need. I have two lengths of red silk in my chest. What difference does it make? What's yours is mine, and what's mine is yours.
Near and dear will always be near and dear.
I give you my body as lovely as a flower,
And my youth like a tender shoot,
In order to share your distinguished career.
I bring a dowry of hundreds of thousands of cash;
I don't mind risking coarse food,
And I don't ask how many other wives you have;
For I'm willing to suffer hardships,
And put up with anything to marry you.
If you go hungry, I'll share your poverty;
If you grow rich, don't discard me as a wanton!
I want you because you please me.
I want you to divorce your present wife,
But not to spend a single cent on me;
I have come to you myself,
Making over my estate to your family,
Making over my good horses and furs to you,
And paying for the wedding into the bargain!
After our marriage you won't find me like Song Yinzhang, who has no idea of wifely duties and knows nothing about cooking, embroidery or sewing.
I'll see that you don't lose out if you divorce her] (Exeunt.)

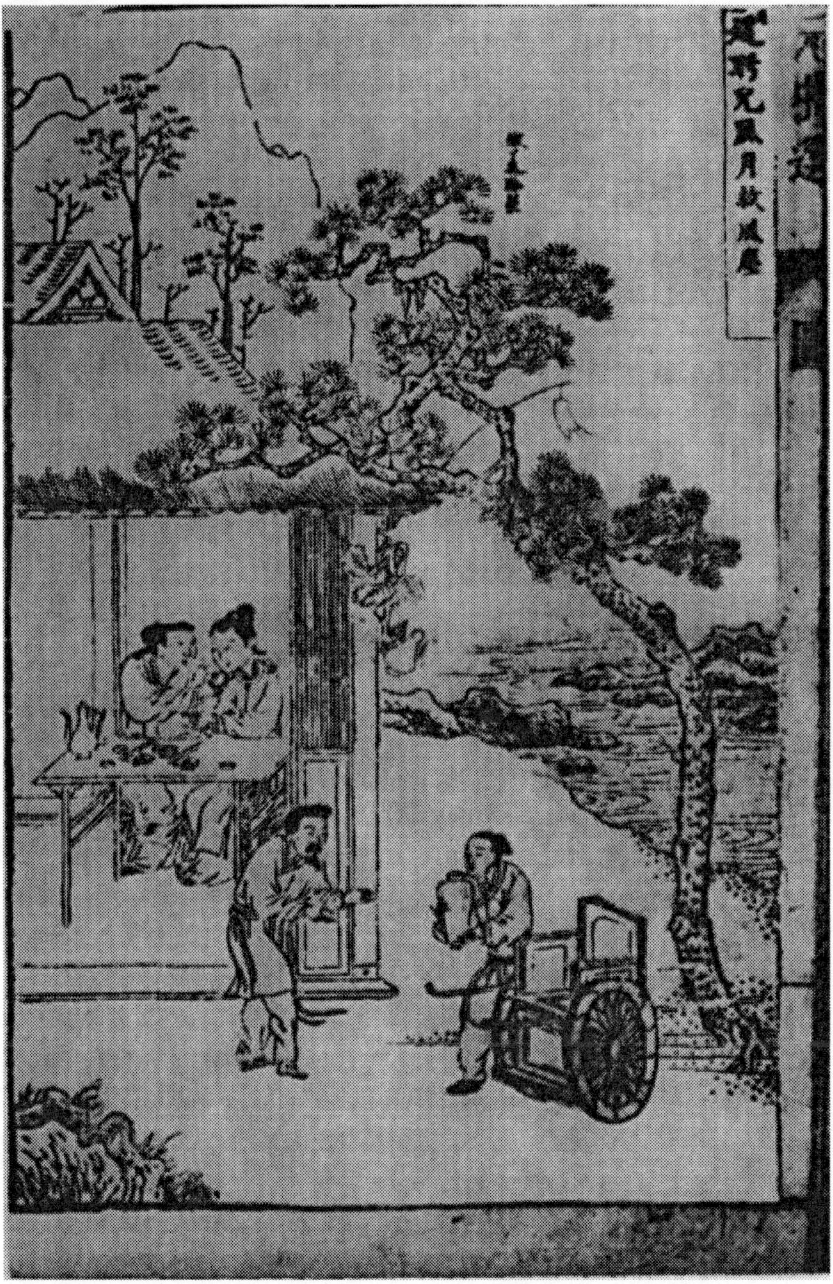

ACT IV

(Enter Yinzhang)

YINZHANG:

Zhou She may be back any time now. *(Enter Zhou She)* Do you want anything to eat or drink?

ZHOU *(angrily):*

A fine wife you are! Here, bring me paper and brush, and I'll write you out a divorce paper. There!
Now be off with you.

YINZHANG *(takes the paper)*:

What have I done wrong that you should divorce me?

ZHOU:

Are you still here? Get out!

YINZHANG:

So you're really divorcing me! *(She goes out)*
At last I've escaped from his clutches. Ah, Zhou She, what a fool you are! And Paner, how clever you are! I shall take this paper straight to the inn to my sister. *(Exit)*

ZHOU:

Now I shall go straight to the inn to marry Paner.
(Exit)
(Enter the Waiter)

WAITER:

Why is Zhou She not here yet?
(Enter Zhou She)

ZHOU:

Boy, where is the girl who arrived not long ago?

WAITER:

She left with her carriage just after you went out.

ZHOU:

    She must have been fooling me! Bring me the mare. I shall catch her up.

WAITER:

    The mare is foaling.

ZHOU:

    Bring me the mule.

WAITER:

    The mule is lame.

ZHOU:

    Bring me the donkey.

WAITER:

    The donkey needs to be shod.

ZHOU:

    Then I'll go after her on foot. *(Exit.)*

WAITER:

    I'll go, too. *(Exit)*
    (Enter Paner and Yinzhang)

YINZHANG:

    If not for you, sister, I could never have got away.

PANER:

    Let's go.
    I smile with pleasure now the divorce is granted.
    Where is our crafty friend now?
    He thinks the world of his charm and cleverness;
    But he is no match for me.

    If you want to marry again, I shall give this divorce paper back to Zhou She. Show me your divorce paper, Yinzhang. When you want to marry, ask for my advice.

    (Zhou She runs in.)

ZHOU *(shouting):*

Stop, you slut! Song Yinzhang, you are my wife! How dare you run away?

YINZHANG:

You gave me a divorce paper, Zhou She, and drove me out.

ZHOU:

There should be five finger-prints on the paper. How can one with four finger-prints be valid?

(Yinzhang takes the paper out to examine it. Zhou snatches it from her, stuffs it into his mouth, and chews it up)

YINZHANG:

He's swallowing my certificate, sister!
(Paner comes back to help her)

ZHOU:

You are my wife too.

PANER:

How can I be your wife?

ZHOU:

You've drunk my wine.

PANER:

I had ten bottles of good wine in my carriage. It was none of yours.

ZHOU:

Well, you accepted my sheep.

PANER:

I had my own cooked sheep. It was none of yours.

ZHOU:

Well, you took my red silk.

PANER:

> I had my own red silk. It was none of yours.
> *You can have the wine and the sheep from my carriage,*
> *And the red silk that I brought;*
> *But lust has made you mad*
> *If you think you can win a wife by such a trick.*

ZHOU:

> Well, you swore an oath to marry me.

PANER:

> *That was simply to fool you.*
> *We singsong girls live by such oaths.*
> If you don't believe me,
> *Ask all the other girls in the courtesans' quarters.*
> *There's not one who will not take a solemn oath,*
> *Calling on Heaven to wipe out her whole clan,*
> *Swearing again and again.*
> *If such oaths came true,*
> *Why, all of us would have perished!*
> Yinzhang, you must go with him.

YINZHANG *(frightened)***:**

> If I go with him, sister, he'll kill me.

PANER:

> *How could you be*
> *So thoughtless and so foolish?*

ZHOU:

> I've destroyed the certificate. Can you refuse to go back with me? *(Yinzhang looks terrified.)*

PANER:

> Don't be afraid, sister. The one he chewed up was a forgery.
> *That was a copy I gave you*
> *But here is the paper itself.*
> *(Zhou tries to snatch it from her.)*
> *Even nine strong bulls couldn't get it away from me!*

ZHOU *(seizing the two girls):*

We'll see what the law says. Come with me to the court! *(Exeunt)*

(Enter the Prefect of Zhengzbou with Attendants.)

PREFECT:

My noble reputation has reached heaven;
At night no household needs to close its doors,
The peasants plough their fields after the rain,
And no dogs bark under the silver moon.

I am Li Kongbi, Prefect of Zhengzhou. Today I am holding a morning session, and shall see what cases there are. Attendants, summon the court!

ATTENDANTS:

Yes, Your Honour!

(Enter Zhou She with the two girls and Mistress Song.)

ZHOU *(shouting):*

Avenge my wrong, Your Honour!

PREFECT:

What is your complaint?

ZHOU:

Your Honour, she has tricked me of my wife.

PREFECT:

Who has?

ZHOU:

Zhao Paner played a trick to get my wife Song Yin-Zhang away from me.

PREFECT:

What have you to say, woman?

PANER:

That cruel scoundrel counts on his wealth,

That false-hearted wretch won't tread the path of virtue.
Yinzhang was betrothed, but he forced her to be his wife!
Bold, wicked, lecherous man,
He does many lawless things wherever he goes.
But here is the deed of divorce.
Please read it, Your Honour!

Your Honour, Song Yinzhang was already betrothed, but Zhou She forced her to marry him. Yesterday he gave her a divorce certificate.

PREFECT:

Who was her betrothed?

PANER:

A scholar named An.

PREFECT:

Zhou She, Song Yinzhang has her own husband. How could you claim she was your wife? This case is very clear. If not for your father's sake, I would send you to gaol. Listen, all of you, to my verdict. Zhou She shall be given sixty strokes with the bastinado, and in future shall be liable to labour conscription like a common citizen. Song Yinzhang shall go back to marry the scholar An. Zhao Paner and the others may go home.

This trouble was caused by the mother's avarice;
Zhao Paner made all things clear;
Zhou She was convicted of gross impropriety;
But the scholar An and his wife are reunited.
(They kowtow to thank the Prefect.)

PANER:

Now all has been explained to His Honour,
And the ill-assorted couple part company;
Do not say that, once married, they should remain together;
But let the love-birds find their mates again!
(THE END)

THE RIVERSIDE PAVILION

CHARACTERS
ABBESS BAI
BAI SHIZHONG, *her nephew, Magistrate of Tanzhou*
TAN JIER, *a young widow*
LORD YANG, *a powerful noble*
YANG'S SERVANT
ZHANG SHAO, *Lord Yang's attendant*
BAI'S ATTENDANT
LI BINGZHONG, *the prefect*
BAI'S STEWARD

ACT I

(Enter Abbess Bai.)

ABBESS:

The law that can be told is not the invariable law;
The names that can be named are not invariable names.

I am Abbess Bai. I entered holy orders as a girl and am now abbess of the Convent of Pure Tranquillity. There's a young woman here called Tan Jier who's as pretty as a picture. But the poor thing's husband has died, leaving her a widow. She comes here every day for a chat. For some years I neither saw nor heard of my nephew Bai Shizhong. Not long ago I was told he'd been made an official, but I haven't seen him yet. Well, we've nothing on today. Let me see who is coming. *(Enter Bai Shizhong.)*

BAI:

All other qualifications count as nothing: Only scholarship wins respect. I have passed the examinations: My name has figured on the Golden List. I am Bai Shizhong, on my way to Tanzhou to take up office. Since my road passes the Convent of Pure Tranquillity, where my aunt is abbess, I shall pay her a call before going on to my post. Here I am at the gate. There is no one to announce me. I may as well go straight in. *(He greets the Abbess)* Aunty, I have been appointed magistrate of Tanzhou, and have broken my journey to pay my respects to you.

ABBESS:

Congratulations, dear nephew! I was just this moment thinking of you, and here you are! How is your wife?

BAI:

Why, aunty, my wife is dead.

ABBESS:

Well, nephew, there's a young lady here called Tan Jier who's a real beauty. She comes every day for a chat. By and by, when she arrives, I'll get her to marry you. What do you say to that?

BAI:

Suppose she isn't willing, aunty?

ABBESS:

Don't worry! You can count on me. Just stay behind the curtain till you hear me cough, then come out.

BAI:

Very well, aunty. *(Exit)*

ABBESS:

Jier should be coming soon.
(Enter Tan Jier.)

TAN:

My name is Tan Jier. I was married to a scholar, Li Xiyan, who died three years ago. I come to this convent every day to see Abbess Bai. Today I have nothing to do, so I will call on her. Ah, it's hard for a woman when she has no one to turn to.

> *The phoenix has lost her mate,*
> *Fragrance has fled my embroidered quilts,*
> *And dusk filled my quiet chamber.*
> *My cheeks bare of rouge and powder,*
> *I grieve through the long, long twilight;*
> *I sigh alone and shed tears*
> *By falling flowers or in the bamboo's shade;*
> *My sighs like a spring breeze make the petals fall,*
> *And my tears stain the emerald rushes.*
> *With my good looks and quick wit*
> *I have mourned for three years as a widow,*
> *My wretchedness as deep as the fathomless sea!*
> *My sorrow knows no bounds:*
> *All men are licentious and lustful,*
> *All out to seduce and trick women.*

Here I am at the convent. There is no one to announce me, so I may as well go straight in. *(She greets the Abbess.)* Ten thousand blessings, mother!

ABBESS:

Please sit down.

TAN:

It is good of you to let me take up your time every day like this. Now I would like to enter holy orders myself. Are you willing to have me?

ABBESS:

How can you become a nun, my dear? Plain clothes and poor fare—ours is a hard life. It is not so bad in the day time, but when evening comes the loneliness is unbearable. You'd do better to marry again.

TAN:

No, mother, you are wrong.
I long for this quiet life,
For then I shall know freedom.
It is hard to live all alone;
I have had my fill of the world
And its many changes of fortune;
All beauty and comfort are nothing but a dream:
Let me join you to seek for the philosopher's stone.

ABBESS:

My dear, I'm afraid you couldn't stomach our vegetarian diet. No, you can't join holy orders.

TAN:

What hardship is there in that?
I am used to plain food.
I shall keep a check on my passionate, mischievous heart,
And renounce all earthly splendour.

ABBESS:

Remember that verse, my dear—*A lonely village in the rain,*

A mountain in the snow,
Although they seem such simple things
Are hard to paint, you know;
And had I guessed such scenes would not
Be popular today,
I would have bought some crimson paint
And painted posies gay!
No, my dear, how can you take orders?

TAN:

You say it is harder than it looks,
But how do you know I cannot live as a nun,
Cannot practise yoga and seek
The philosopher's stone?

ABBESS:

With your looks, my dear, you can easily find a man you fancy and marry him. Why choose such a hard life?

TAN:

If I could find a man who would love me as much as my last husband, I would consider it.

(The Abbess coughs. Bai comes in and greets the girl.)

BAI:

Good day!
(Tan returns his greeting.)

TAN:

Since you have a guest, mother, I will leave you now.

ABBESS:

Don't go, my dear! What do you say to taking this man as your husband?

TAN:

Mother, what a thing to say!

> *How could you take a chance remark so seriously?*
> *We have scarcely met, yet you talk like a go-between!*

ABBESS:

After all, you have been married once.

TAN:

> *How can you imply*
> *That I would take a lover?*

ABBESS:

The gate is shut and I won't let you go!

TAN:

> *So now you shut me in!*
> *You dare bring this stranger to vex me!*
> *Do you think me a loose woman,*
> *That you hide this man in your convent*
> *And stop me from leaving?*
> *For three years we have been friends,*
> *But this is the end of our friendship.*
> *You have been an abbess all these years for nothing.*

ABBESS:

Why shouldn't the two of you become man and wife?

TAN:

> *You will spoil the reputation of your convent:*
> *People will start to despise you,*
> *You ought to keep this nunnery clean and chaste,*
> *Attend to your stove and sutras,*
> *And not complain so much of your lonely life!*

ABBESS:

Who told you to come here, sir?

BAI:

This young lady.

TAN:

How dare you! I would rather die than marry you!

ABBESS:

Do you want this settled in court or out of court?

TAN:

What do you mean?

ABBESS:

If you want it settled in court, I'll report it to the authorities. You've no right to carry on like this in our convent, bringing a man here to drag our name through the mud. You'll be tried and given a beating. If you want it settled out of court—you are a girl, he is a young man, and I am your go-between. That is much the better way.

TAN:

Let me think it over, mother.

ABBESS:

So a thousand prayers are less use than one threat!

TAN:

What a fine abbess—so good at blackmail! I'll marry him on two conditions, mother. Not otherwise.

BAI:

I'd agree to ten conditions, let alone two.

TAN:

I'll agree to marry him
If he promises never to leave me,
And to remember the saying:
A just rule accords with Heaven,
A good official gives the people peace.
Let him live up to this!
And I must congratulate you
For finding time to make matches between your sutras;
Remaining in the hills like a statesman of old,

You manage affairs outside from your quiet retreat.
Well, mother, let me say this—
Though your convent's name is Pure Tranquillity,
You seem an experienced matchmaker!
All the love-sick and lonely
Should come to you for medicine,
And you can give them this treatment;
For surely you are an expert
In curing loneliness and sleeplessness!
Very well, mother. I'll do as you say and accept his offer.

ABBESS:

Well, nephew, you ought to thank me for this.

TAN:

Yes, surely you are an expert in curing loneliness and sleeplessness! I do thank you, aunty. After I've been to my new post, I'll thank you properly.

AN:

Since you have to go to your post, let us say goodbye now and set out.

BAI:

Very well, ma'am.

ABBESS:

Take good care of yourself on the journey, dear nephew. You make a capital pair—a talented scholar and a beautiful girl.

TAN:

Let us start with no more delay,
Lest pursuers overtake us;
But if any man pursues me
He shall not see my face.
You need not warn us, aunty. Rest assured!
Pull in the boat, pull out the stake, step aboard!
Hoist sail and scud before the autumn wind!
As clouds alight upon the river banks,

Our light craft races past ten thousand hills.
(Exeunt Tan and Bai.)

ABBESS:

Well! Today I have found my nephew an excellent wife! I *am* pleased! I've nothing to do now—I may as well go and ask our patrons for alms.

I didn't impose on her,
But feared trouble might come to my convent
If she remained a young widow;
That's why I tricked her into taking my nephew! (Exit)

ACT II

(Enter Lord Yang.)

YANG:

I am the rake of rakes,
First among profligates.
All citizens fear me—
The powerful Lord Yang! I am Lord Yang. When I heard of the beauty of Li Xiyan's widow, Tan Jier, I tried to make her my concubine. But now that dog Bai Shizhong has married her on his way to Tanzhou, where he is magistrate. The abbess of the Convent of Pure Tranquillity was their go-between. Well, a gentleman knows how to hate. A stout fellow does nothing by halves. I am not going to stand for this. He has no call to envy me, but I envy him. So I told the emperor today that Bai neglects public business for wine and women. When His Majesty issued an order for his execution, I immediately urged him not to send anyone else, but to let me go in person to cut off Bai's head—then there could be no mistake. His Majesty has agreed and given me the sword of authority and gold tally. Now, attendant, tell my two men to get the boat ready. We're going straight to Tanzhou to cut off Bai's head.

I weigh this matter well:
I meant Tan Jier to be mine
But she married another man.
Well, soon I shall cut off his head! (Exit.) (Enter Bai.)

BAI:

Since I came to this post, I have won the people's heart and every man under my jurisdiction can go about his work in peace. My wife is very able, and has proved a great help to me. Lord Yang wanted to make her his concubine, but instead she became my wife. Beside being so virtuous, she is most brilliant and accomplished—I have never seen another woman like her. But I hear Lord Yang bears me a grudge, and I am afraid he means to harm me. This is preying on my mind. This morning's court session is over and I have nothing to do. I will rest a little here in the front hall, so that my wife does not see how worried I am. *(Enter an old Steward.)*

STEWARD:

> *An old servant, I work hard*
> *For the house of Bai.*
> *The old lady has ordered me*
> *To warn the young master.*

I am an old steward of the Bai family. My master, Bai Shizhong, is magistrate of Tanzhou, but Lord Yang has slandered him to the emperor, who has ordered Lord Yang to cut off my master's head. Our old mistress got word of this, and has sent me to Tanzhou to warn her son. Here I am at last. I must give him the letter. I won't wait to be announced, but go straight in. *(He bows to Bai)* Greetings, sir.

BAI:

What brings you here?

STEWARD:

The old lady ordered me to bring you this letter.

BAI:

A letter from my mother? Let me see it.

STEWARD *(handing him the letter):*

Here it is. *(Bai reads the letter)*

BAI:

Very well, I understand. So that scoundrel is plotting against me as I suspected. Go in and have a meal.

STEWARD:

Thank you, sir. *(Exit)*

BAI:

So Lord Yang bears me such a grudge for marrying Tan Jier that he has slandered me to the emperor in order to have me killed. What can I do? Let me think this over. Ah, I hear someone coming. *(Enter Tan)*

TAN:

Since my husband came to this post he has won the people's heart. After each morning court he usually comes to me in the inner hall. He is late today. I must go and see what has happened.

I hear no runners shouting—
Can he still be holding court?
I should have heard of an official visit,
And I doubt if there is any emergency.
I wonder what this means.
I step to the screen to have a look—
There he is, alone and dejected.

I had better have a look before going in. Ah, he has a sheet of paper in his hand and is poring over it. Now I understand.

Though the proverb says:
Men's secrets die with them,
Even the ocean bed lies revealed at last.
He must have another wife,
Who has learned of his marriage to me
And sent him this letter.
He left his old wife for a new one,
Marrying me by a trick!

Since there is no one to announce me, I'll go straight in. *(She greets Bai.)* Sir!

BAI:

Why have you come here, my love?

TAN:

Why didn't you join me? Has your first wife written to you?

BAI:

How can you suspect such a thing, my dear! No, I am worried by some public business.

TAN:

Don't try to deceive me. You must have another wife at home, who has written to you now.

BAI:

How can you be so suspicious? I would never deceive you.

TAN:

You must be faithful to your wife;
Why should you take more women than one?
So now you are in a quandary.
Well, keep the one you prefer
And abandon the other.
It is you who must make the decision.

BAI:

It really is public business, and I hope it will not prevent my living to a great age with you. I swear before Heaven I shall always be true to you, and I have no other wife.

TAN:

What was that paper I saw in your hand? It must be a letter from your wife at home. Don't try to deceive me. I can guess what is in it.

BAI:

Well, what is your guess?

TAN:

It is hard to abandon your first wife,
But easy to deal with the second,
For she is simply a casual love,
While the first is your wife betrothed to you in childhood.
Though merely a simple woman,
I can guess what is in a man's mind
By the slightest movement of his eyes or head.
I am not trying to display my intelligence!
Ah, sir, I will leave you when you tell me to,

Without waiting till our love burns out,
Till we turn our faces away from each other;
Till the lake dries up and the wild geese fly apart.

BAI:

I am not so heartless, my dear. How could I have another wife?

TAN:

Why won't you tell me the truth?

BAI:

I have no other wife—what do you expect me to say?

TAN:

If you won't tell me, I shall kill myself.

BAI:

Wait! Wait! What should I do without you? I'll tell you if you insist, but you must promise not to worry.

TAN:

If you tell me the truth, I shan't worry.

BAI:

Very well. You know Lord Yang wanted to have you as his concubine, but I married you instead. Because he bears me a grudge, he has slandered me to the emperor, saying I neglect public business for wine and women. Now His Majesty has given him the sword of authority and gold tally, and he is coming to Tanzhou to cut off my head. An old steward brought this letter from my mother to warn me of my danger. That is what was on my mind.

TAN:

So that is it! Why should you be afraid of him?

BAI:

The scoundrel is a powerful man, my dear.

TAN:

What if he is?
He can hardly take another man's wife by force.
The fellow has no sense of propriety,
But only tries to gratify his lust.
So mark my words:
I shall never yield to him;
His advantages will work to his disadvantage;
He will have to slink back empty-handed.
Stop beating your breast and lamenting]
I shall go in plain costume
With unlacquered eyebrows,
I shall go today
And see what he means to do.

BAI:

No, no! You mustn't go.

TAN:

Don't worry, sir. Listen! *(She whispers to him)*
What do you say to that?

BAI:

But you may fall into his trap.

TAN:

Don't be afraid.
I shall make him kowtow to me
Like a bleating lamb.
On his boat in midstream
I shall steal his gold tally from him
And leave him no way out! (Exit)

BAI:

So my wife has gone. She is so intelligent that a hundred Lord Yangs could not escape her, let alone one!
The army has gone into battle,
And I wait here for good tidings. (Exit)

ACT III

(Enter Lord Yang with Zhang Shao and another servant)

YANG:

I am Lord Yang. Let's see you escape me now, Bai Shizhong—curse you! I recommended you for this post, but I wanted Tan Jier for my concubine. How could I tell that he would turn against me and marry her behind my back? That was too much! I have come to Tanzhou to cut off his head. Why did I only bring Zhang Shao and one other man with me? Because they're clever rogues who can be trusted. That's why I brought them.

(The Servant plucks at Lord Yang's hair)

YANG:

Hey, what are you doing?

SERVANT:

There was a louse in your hair, sir.

YANG:

The fellow may be right. I have been on this boat for a month and not combed my hair. Good lad!

(Zhang plucks at Lord Yang's hair)

YANG:

Hey, Zhang Shao, what are you doing?

ZHANG:

Sir, there was a tick in your hair.

YANG:

Devil take it!

(The Servant and Zhang both snatch at Lord Yang's hair)

YANG:

Steady on, boys. How can there be so many?

ZHANG:

I say! Today is the fifteenth of the eighth month—the Moon Festival. Let's prepare some wine and sweetmeats so that our master can enjoy the moonlight. How about it?

SERVANT:

Right. Let's suggest it to him. *(They bow to Yang)*

YANG:

What do you want?

ZHANG:

Sir, today is the Moon Festival and there is bright moonlight. We want to prepare a little wine to celebrate the festival.

YANG *(angrily)*:

Are you raving? I am here on public business—how can you expect me to drink?

SERVANT:

We meant well, sir. We just wanted to show our respect. You drink. We won't touch a drop.

YANG:

Ha! What if you break your word?

SERVANT:

If I drink so much as a drop, may the wine turn to blood!

YANG:

Good. You mustn't drink. How about you, Zhang Shao?

ZHANG:

If I drink, may I break out in boils!

YANG:

All right, since the two of you aren't going to drink, I'll have a few cups. Get the wine and sweetmeats ready.

SERVANT:

Bring out the tray, Zhang Shao.

ZHANG *(fetching the tray):*

Here it is. I'll hold the wine pot while you pass the wine.

SERVANT:

Yes, fill the cup. *(He holds out the cup)* Drink up, sir. *(As Lord Yang reaches for the cup, the Servant turns away and drinks the wine himself)*

YANG:

What do you think you're doing?

SERVANT:

I'm testing it for poison, sir. We didn't bring this wine with us but bought it outside. If you were to drink it and get poisoned, what should we do?

YANG:

Quite right. You're a good fellow.

ZHANG *(passing the wine)*:

You made that up because you wanted a drink. Sir, have a cup of wine. *(Before Lord Yang can take the cup, Zhang drains it)*

YANG:

Hey! Why are *you* drinking it now?

ZHANG:

If he can drink, sir, so can I.

YANG:

Curse you! Let me have a few cups now in peace while you drive away the other boats. There is someone coming.

(Enter Tan carrying a fish)

TAN:

There is no one here. I am Tan Jier, the wife of Bai Shizhong. I have dressed myself like a fishwife to see Lord Yang. A fine fish this is! It was frisking along with the waves looking for food, when I launched my boat, cast my net and caught it. Glittering scales, three feet long! It will be very tasty, sliced. A beautiful fish!

Tonight is a festival,
There should be singing and drinking
Before the flowers fade and the moon wanes;
The tables are spread with dainties,
But nothing is so delicious as this fish;
No need to boil or fry it—
Simply cut it into thin slices.
It is not easy to come here.
I am using this fish to approach;
May some generous customer buy it.
This is not the usual fish sold in the market;
With one net, straw coat and straw hat,
I have come on special business;
May I find good customers!

I moor my boat and step ashore. *(She greets Zhang.)* Good evening.

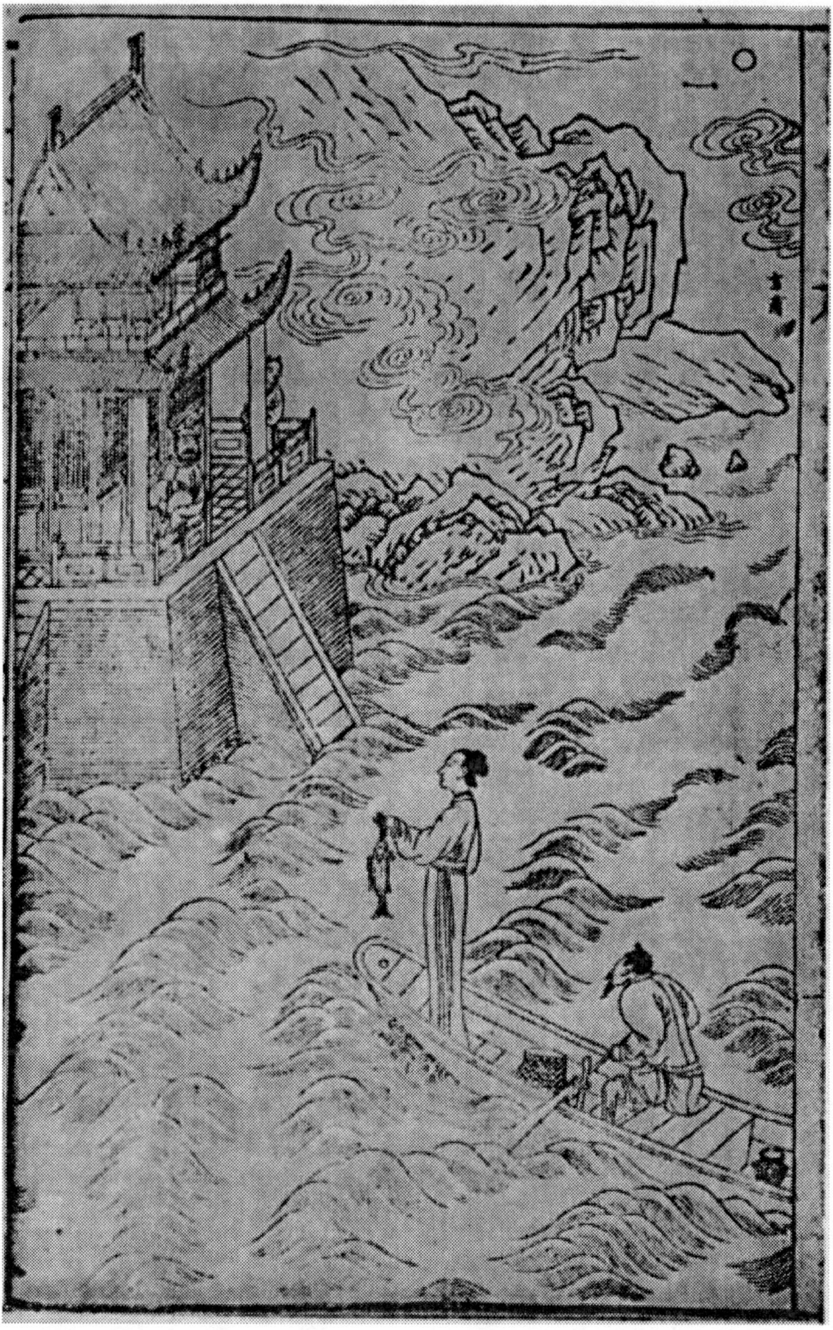

ZHANG:

I seem to know you, sister.

TAN:

Who do you think I am?

ZHANG:

Aren't you Mrs. Zhang?

TAN:

Of course. How could you forget me? But who are you?

ZHANG:

I'm Tortoise Zhang, of course.

TAN:

That's it! *(She slaps him.)* Darling boy! These days I can see you have been eating well. I often think of you.

ZHANG:

Do you love me, sister?

TAN:

Of course, son. Now go and tell your master that I'm going to slice some fish for him, so that I can make a little money.

ZHANG:

Sure. Here, you!

SERVANT:

What do you want?

ZHANG:

There's a Mrs. Zhang here who wants to slice some fish for our master.

SERVANT:

What Mrs. Zhang?

TAN *(greeting the Servant):*

To show my respect, I have brought a golden carp to give your master. Please put in a word for me.

SERVANT:

All right, I will, if you'll give me some of the money to buy a drink. Come on.

(To Lord Yang.) Sir, a Mrs. Zhang here wants to slice some fish for you.

YANG:

What Mrs. Zhang?

TAN *(greeting Lord Yang):*

Good evening, Your Honour.
YANG *(admiring her):* A fine-looking woman!

SERVANT:

A nice lady!

ZHANG:

A real bitch!

YANG:

What brought you here, ma'am?

TAN:

To show my respect, I have brought you this golden carp. If you'll let me have a knife and chopping board, I'll slice it for you.

YANG:

That's very good of you, but I can't have you soiling your hands with that. Zhang Shao, take it and fry it with ginger and pepper.

ZHANG:

Better let her do it, sir.

YANG:

    Thank you for coming here, my good woman. Here, fellow, bring some sweetmeats. I'll drink a few cups with this young woman. Pour out the wine. Drink it, ma'am!
(The Servant drinks the wine.)

YANG:

    What are you doing?

SERVANT:

    Are you going to drink or not? You just press each other.

YANG:

    Hold your tongue and get out of the way. Bring more wine. *(To Tan.)* Drink this cup.

TAN:

    After you, Your Honour!

SERVANT:

    Go on! If you won't drink, I will.
(Tan kneels to Lord Yang, who helps her up.)

YANG:

    Please sit down, ma'am. If I let you kneel to me, how can we be lovers?

TAN:

    Now that I'm here, even if you let me kneel to you we can still be lovers.

ZHANG and SERVANT:

    Wonderful, wonderful!

YANG:

    Please be seated, ma'am.

TAN:

    Where are you going, Your Honour?

YANG:

I am travelling on public business.

ZHANG:

He's here to kill Bai Shizhong, Mrs. Zhang.

YANG:

Hold your tongue!

TAN:

If Your Honour arrests Bai Shizhong, that will be one rogue the less. But how is it the prefecture hasn't sent men to welcome you?

YANG:

You don't understand—I don't want word to leak out.

TAN:

Had you announced your arrival,
You could have feasted on board
With dozens of musicians.
Coming on government business,
Why need you travel in secret?

YANG:

It's a good thing you came early, ma'am. If you'd come any later, I should have gone to bed.

TAN:

Yes, had I come any later,
You would have been sound asleep,
With your sword of authority and gold tally by you.
All seeing an official would have kept away
With no need for attendants to guard you.
And I, who came to do business,
Would surely have had a stick broken across my back!

YANG:

Zhang Shao, do me a favour and be my go-between. Tell Mrs. Zhang she can't be my wife, but I'll take her as my concubine. She shall have a shawl, silk smock and embroidered handkerchief.

ZHANG:

Don't worry, sir. You can depend on me.
(To Tan.) Mrs. Zhang, you are in luck. You heard what our master said. You can't be his wife, but he'll take you as his concubine, and give you a shawl, silk smock and border chief....

TAN:

You mean an embroidered handkerchief.

ZHANG:

That's right.

TAN:

I can't believe it. I'll ask him for myself.
(To Yang.)
Sir, is what Zhang Shao said just now true?

YANG:

Yes, that's what I said.

TAN:

Who am I to deserve such an honour?

YANG:

All right, all right. Won't you sit next to me? It doesn't matter.

TAN:

You are doing me a great honour.
I will not boast of my chastity,
But this is the first time I have fallen in love.
Though I am plain, and a little rude and stubborn,
At the sight of you I cannot hold myself back
Or put up any resistance.

> *You have come, sir, to rescue the people,*
> *Take no half measures then—*
> *When you catch that wicked magistrate*
> *You must see that blood is spilt!*
> *I am longing to share your bed:*
> *I cannot be pure as snow or cold as ice.*
> *(Tan Jier glances at him significantly.)*

YANG *(pleased):*

Well, well!

ZHANG and SERVANT *(echoing him):*

Well, well!

YANG:

What are you two doing?

ZHANG:

Joining in the fun.

TAN:

> *I shall have a pearl-decked head-dress,*
> *Bright silks, gay canopy,*
> *And maids to wait on me!*
> *My bones ache from rowing a boat,*
> *But now I shall enjoy a comfortable carriage.*

YANG:

Let us compose a couplet together, ma'am.
Her silk sleeve overturns the cockatoo cup.

TAN:

My slender fingers fold the phoenix bedding.

SERVANT and ZHANG *(banging the table):*

Wonderful, wonderful!

YANG:

I suppose you can read and write?

TAN:

> A little.

YANG:

> Then let's compose another couplet.
> *The cock-head[21] seed cannot stretch its neck.*

TAN:

> *The dragon-eye[22] fruit cannot turn its glance.*

ZHANG and SERVANT *(banging the table):*

> Wonderful, wonderful!

TAN:

> Zhang Shao, let me make a couplet with you.

ZHANG:

> Of course! We'd make a fine couple.

TAN:

> Hold your tongue!
> *Storks fly in pairs through the sky—*

ZHANG:

> *Lovers sleep together on earth.*

TAN:

> Your Honour, may I ask you to write a poem?

YANG:

> All right. Zhang Shao, bring pen, paper and ink.

ZHANG *(bringing them):*

> Here they are, sir.

---

[21] A kind of water-lily.

[22] A fruit also known as Longan.

YANG:

It is done. This is to the tune "Moonlight on the Western River."

TAN:

Do read it to me, Your Honour!

YANG *(reading):*

The chill dew falls, the moonlight gleams,
The autumn wind sweeps lakes and streams.
Let lovely maid a blossom hold,
My inmost thoughts cannot be told;
Descended from the sky by night,
She knows my heart—for her I write.

TAN:

What genius! I shall reply with another poem to the tune of "Sailing at Night."

YANG:

Read it to me, ma'am.

TAN *(reading):*

Two birds beneath the blooms are better than a lonely phoenix:
This sudden romance of ours was surely predestined,
Like the fish and water we,
The lake is cold but, with the moon as companion,
We sail our boat through the night.

YANG:

Wonderful, wonderful! Let's drink a few more cups, ma'am.

TAN:

Why do you want to kill Bai Shizhong, Your Honour?

YANG:

You mustn't ask me that.

ZHANG:

    Mrs. Zhang, our master has the sword of authority here.

YANG:

    Don't show it!

TAN:

    So this is the sword of authority. Will you lend it to me for a couple of days to slice fish?

YANG:

    All right.

SERVANT:

    And here is the gold tally.

TAN:

    So this is the gold tally. Will you give it me to make gold rings? What else have you got?

ZHANG:

    Here is the imperial edict.

TAN:

    This is only a business contract. *(She slips it into her sleeve.)* Drink another cup, Your Honour.

YANG:

    I've had enough. Just sing the last part of your poem, ma'am. *(He falls into a drunken stupor.)*

TAN:

The lake is cold but, with the moon as companion,
We sail our boat through the night.
(Zhang and the Servant fall asleep too.)
Now they are all asleep.
Fools, there they lie in a heap,
Their eyes heavy with sleep and wine;
Tucking the tally in my sleeve,

I wish them a rude awakening,
And make a deep bow to Lord Yang.
My skiff will soon take me home
To tell my husband all that has happened here,
And this will make him glad.
What a stroke of luck!
Holding gold goblets,
We shall enjoy the moon;
Hand in hand we shall drink,
Leaning close to each other,
While Lord Yang sleeps alone in his boat. (Exit.)

YANG:

Where is Mrs. Zhang? *(Startled.)*

ZHANG:

Where has she gone? Where is the gold tally?

SERVANT:

The gold tally isn't the only thing that has gone The sword and edict have disappeared too.

ZHANG:

I stamp my feet in dismay!

SERVANT:

Here's a fine to-do!

YANG:

I am burning with secret rage!

TOGETHER:

But we dare not let anyone know.
Let us go to offer incense,
And lay a curse on that woman!

ZHANG:

The sun has set and we have nowhere to go.

SERVANT:
>Where shall I sleep tonight?

YANG:
>These rogues are singing southern opera![23] *(Exeunt.)*

---

[23] In the southern opera several characters sometimes sang together.

ACT IV

(Enter Bai Shizhong with his Attendant)

BAI:

Here are no quarrels, and little conscript labour;
All my people are happy and live at peace.

I am Bai Shizhong. There is no public business today. Let me see who is coming.

(Enter Lord Yang with his Servant and Zhang Shao.)

YANG:

I am Lord Yang. I am going to get Bai Shizhong's head. Here is the gate. Let's go in. *(He sees Bai.)* Men, arrest Bai Shizhong.

SERVANT *(going to seize Bai):*

Yes, Your Honour.

BAI:

Where is your warrant for my arrest?

YANG:

I have an imperial edict. Let me read it to you. *(Reading)* To the tune of "Moonlight on the Western River...."

BAI *(snatching the paper):*

This is an indecent poem!

YANG:

That's not the one. Here it is. *(Reading)* To the tune of "Sailing by Night."

BAI *(snatching the paper):*

Another indecent poem!"

YANG:

This wretch has turned the tables on me. Well, never mind. As there is no charge against me, I have nothing to fear.

BAI:

I wish someone would come and lay a charge against him.
(Enter Tan dressed as a fisherwoman)

TAN:

I am Tan Jier, Bai Shizhong's wife. That scoundrel Lord Yang has done me a great wrong.
*Was there ever official so corrupt
As this bully, so inflamed by wine and women!
He wanted to seduce a married woman,
And tried to use his power
To separate husband and wife.
He has used me most unjustly—
Protect the poor, Your Honour! (She kneels to Bai)*

Have pity, Your Honour! Lord Yang tried to seduce me on the river. I demand justice.

BAI:

Go to the clerks' office and write down your plea.

TAN:

Yes, Your Honour. *(Exit.)*

BAI:

So there is a charge against you after all, Lord Yang. Now what do you say?

YANG:

What ever shall I do? I'll try to get on the good side of him. Sir, listen to me.

BAI:

What is it?

YANG:

I am willing to let you off, if you will let me off. But I have one request to make. I have heard much praise of your wife—I should like to meet her.

BAI:
>Very well. Attendant, ask my lady to come out.

ATTENDANT:
>Yes, Your Honour. Madam, His Honour wants you.
>*(Enter Tan in different dress.)*

TAN:
>Now I shall see what that fellow will do.
>*He is too stunned to speak.*
>*I have heard of your fame as a profligate,*
>*And am honoured to meet you today.*
>*Accept my greetings, my lord.*

YANG:
>I seem to have seen this lady before.

ZHANG:
>Isn't she Mrs. Zhang?

YANG:
>Ah, madam, that was a fine trick you played. You took me in completely!

TAN:
>*He is speechless with surprise.*
>*We cannot have him beaten or thrown into gaol,*
>*For between him and me*
>*There passed simply a few words.*
>*Half a night on a fishing-boat*
>*Has won us joy at this Moon Festival.*
>*(Enter Li Bingzhong the prefect.)*

PREFECT:
>*On my black charger I gallop to Tanzhou.*
>I am Li Bingzhong, the prefect. After Lord Yang made a false report, the government sent me here to find out the truth.

Now I have come to Tanzhou and learned all about you both—Bai Shizhong and Lord Yang. Listen now to my verdict!
Lord Yang abused his power
And accused a good officer wrongly;
Tan Jier is a clever woman,
Who tricked him out of the tally to save her husband.
I was sent by the government to investigate.
Lord Yang shall lose his official post;
Let a feast be spread to celebrate,
And may Bai Shizhong and his wife
Live happily hereafter!
(THE END)

THE JADE MIRROR-STAND

CHARACTERS
MISTRESS LIU, *an old widow*
QIANYING, *her daughter*
WEN JIAO, *an academician, Mistress Liu's nephew*
MEIXIANG, *a maidservant*
MATCHMAKER
PREFECT WANG
ATTENDANTS

ACT I

(Enter Mistress Liu with Meixiang.)

MRS. LIU:

Flowers may bloom again,
But youth will never return.
Do not count gold a treasure:
Happiness is more precious.

My maiden name is Wen. My husband's name was Liu. He died before his time, leaving me with no son but with one daughter—Qianying. She is eighteen now, but not yet engaged. When my husband was alive he taught her to read and write, but she is not very accomplished yet. Now I want her to learn calligraphy and the lyre. She needs a good tutor though. My nephew Wen Jiao, who is a member of the Hanlin Academy, has invited us to move into his old house in the capital and promised to call; but so far his work has kept him too busy. Last night the lamp sputtered, and this morning I heard magpies cry.[24] Keep your eye on the gate, girl, and let me know who is coming.

MEIXIANG:

Yes, ma'am.
(Enter Wen Jiao)

WEN:

I am Wen Jiao, a scholar of the Hanlin Academy. My only relative is an old aunt who is a widow, whom I recently asked to come and live in the capital. These last few days I have been too busy with public affairs to call, but today I have time to pay my respects to her. Now that we have a wise ruler, men of talent are promoted, and wealth and official rank seem easy to win. But it has always been the way that some scholars have realized their ambitions while others have failed. As for those who succeed—

High carriages throng their gates,

---

[24] These were signs of good luck.

Humble visitors wait at their doors,
They discuss affairs of state,
And their word is law.
They feast in sumptuous style,
And such is their fame that strangers
Bow to them in the street;
They travel with a handsome equipage,
Live in magnificent mansions,
Give orders potent as the thunderbolt,
Write with the brilliance of the stars in heaven;
Armed guards precede them, servants go behind,
And everything they may desire is theirs.
Their smile makes sparrows flaunt like phoenixes,
Their frown makes tigers cringe;
In life they are beyond the reach of the law,
In death their portraits hang for all to see;
Theirs are many fiefs and titles,
Generals they are, and princes. And then there are the failures—
White-haired, ineffectual scholars
Year after year take the examinations,
And study by the window in poor light.
Will they never be appointed
A minister or commander?
They long for a sage monarch's prosperous reign,
When gold nets are cast far and wide
To gather in all good men.
In ancient times the sovereign sought for talent,
And King Tang had a happy reign
Because he went to Youxin to find ministers.
Fu Yue was a humble mason,
Yi Yin a peasant working in the fields,
Country fellows both of them.
And not all good men do well.
Confucius was a king without a throne,
Whose teachings influenced the entire world.
From him his disciples learned

The rules of morality.
He travelled from his native place
By carriage to different states;
He was a teacher of kings,
The guide of all men—
But in the State of Chen he nearly starved.
Mencius also had to wander
Through the States of Ji and Liang,
And all men know how the kings Zhou and Jie
Killed the wise Bi Kan and Long Peng.
Qu Yuan was driven to drown himself,
The Duke of Zhou prayed to Heaven,
But not till they opened the golden casket
Did King Cheng know his loyalty.[25]
I would not say I am boastful.
I am now enjoying fame,
Wealth and nobility;
My forbears were eminent men,
The elders of my clan have a good name,
And the younger members serve as ministers.
We are constantly at court,
Continually beside the golden steps;
But my gilded chamber and painted hall are empty,
I wake lonely after drinking
And pass the spring days in boredom,
Saddened by the breeze and the moon.
Shall I never hold a bride in my arms,
And drown all my cares in the pleasures
Of the curtained wedding bed?

---

[25] The *Book of History* relates that when King Wu fell ill, the Duke of Zhou prayed to die in his place, putting his prayer in a golden casket. After Cheng became king the Duke of Zhou was accused of trying to usurp the throne; but when the king opened the casket and found the prayer, he realized the duke's loyalty.

While talking to myself, I have reached my aunt's house. Girl! Go and tell your mistress that Wen Jiao is at the gate.

MEIXIANG:

Yes, sir. *(Announcing him)* The academician is at the gate, ma'am.

MRS. LIU:

I was just talking of him, and here he is. Ask him to come in.

MEIXIANG:

Please come in, sir.
(Wen greets Mistress Liu.)

MRS. LIU:

You must be very busy with affairs of state. Draw up a seat, girl, and ask the gentleman to sit down. Then pour him some wine.

MEIXIANG:

Here is the wine, sir.

MRS. LIU:

Please drink one cup.
(Wen drinks the wine.)

MRS. LIU:

Meixiang, tell your young mistress to come out and meet our guest.

MEIXIANG:

Yes, ma'am. You are wanted, young mistress!
(Enter Qianying.)

QIANYING:

I was sewing in my room when Meixiang told me my mother wanted me in the front hall. What can she want me for? Let me go and find out. *(She greets Mistress Liu.)* Why did you send for me, mother?

MRS. LIU:

I want you to pay your respects to your cousin, child.

QIANYING:

Yes, mother.

MRS. LIU:

Wait one minute. Meixiang, fetch the master's silver-inlaid armchair from the front, and ask the gentleman to sit in it while the young mistress pays her respects.

WEN:

How can I presume to sit in my uncle's chair?

MRS. LIU:

Please don't stand on ceremony, but do as I say.

WEN:

Very well, aunt.

MRS. LIU:

Now, Qianying, pay your respects to your cousin.

QIANYING:

Yes, mother.
(Qianying curtseys, and Wen bows from his seat.)

MRS. LIU:

When your younger cousin pays her respects, why should you bow to her?

WEN:

All courtesies should be returned. How can I sit here and make no acknowledgement?

MRS. LIU:

What a charming man!

WEN *(aside):*

What a beautiful girl!

> *My soul is taking flight,*
> *My eyes are dazzled!*
> *She is an angel from heaven,*
> *Powdered, rouged and scented,*
> *With tinkling pendants of jade,*
> *And gauzy, new, heavenly garments,*
> *Yet her charm is still her own.*
> *Nothing can add to it; no one*
> *Could remain unmoved by her;*
> *Even a heart of iron*
> *She would surely break!*
> *I devour her with my eyes—*
> *Flowers are not so lovely as her cheeks,*
> *Jade not so fair as her skin.*
> *When the poet Song Yu wrote*
> *Of King Xiang and his dream of the goddess,*
> *Imagined delights in the tower day and night*
> *Made him fall mortally ill;*
> *Were he here beside her now*
> *His bones would melt—*
> *He would perish utterly.*

MRS. LIU:

Bring the wine, Meixiang. Offer your cousin a cup, Qianying.

QIANYING *(presenting the wine):*

Cousin, please drink some wine.

WEN *(taking the cup):*

> Though the cup is light, how can
> Such slender fingers hold it?
> I should not keep a fairy standing so long!
> Treated as her elder brother,
> I am too confused to reply,
> And spill half my wine on the steps.

MRS. LIU:

I want her to learn calligraphy and to play the lyre, but I cannot find a good tutor. I hope, for my sake, you will teach her to write and play.

WEN:

Why, aunty, unskilled as I am, how can I teach her?

MRS. LIU:

Don't be over-modest. Meixiang, fetch the calendar, and let the gentleman choose a lucky day to begin lessons.

WEN:

When I came out today I looked up the calendar for other reasons, and found that tomorrow is an auspicious day.
There is nothing amiss tomorrow;
It is an auspicious day for our family,
Not a day of evil comets to be avoided.
The calendar is a sure guide—
Some days are propitious,
Others ill-starred and unlucky.

MRS. LIU:

Don't be too modest.

WEN:

Certainly, ma'am, I shall come tomorrow. But I do not know enough to teach the young lady.

MRS. LIU:

Don't refuse now. Teach her for her father's sake if not for mine.

WEN:

The days are so short,
Would I could teach her all night!
I would gladly abandon my post
In order to be her teacher.

> *Only one thing is needed—*
> *Let a quiet study be prepared for us!*

MRS. LIU:

Child, you may go back to your chamber after you have said goodbye to your cousin.

QIANYING:

Yes, mother. *(She curtseys and goes out.)*

MRS. LIU:

It is very good of you to accept her as your pupil. I hope you will come early tomorrow.

WEN:

> Indeed I will, ma'am.
> *She stood there like a spray of cherry blossom,*
> *Holding the fragrant wine,*
> *Filling my heart with sorrow*
> *And making me drunk with her beauty.*
> *I walk down the steps in a daze,*
> *Leaving the wonders of the painted hall;*
> *Just now the setting sun hung over the willows,*
> *Now dark clouds cover the sky;*
> *We shall sit together by the green gauze window,*
> *But when night falls*
> *I shall lie alone in the gloom;*
> *And rain dripping from the eaves*
> *Will only increase my despair. (Exit.)*

MRS. LIU:

Get the library ready, Meixiang. Tomorrow is a lucky day, and we have asked the academician to teach the young mistress to play the lyre and write. When you have cleaned the room out, let me know. *(Exit)*

MEIXIANG:

I must do as I am told. Let me go to tell my young lady and to get the study ready. *(Exit)*

ACT II

(Enter Mistress Liu.)

MRS. LIU:

Yesterday we decided that this was a lucky day.
Go and watch at the gate, Meixiang. Let me know when the tutor comes.

MEIXIANG:

Yes, ma'am.
(Enter Wen.)

WEN:

As my aunt decided I should start teaching today, I did not go to my office. She sent again to remind me, but I should have come in any case. Here is her gate. Please announce me, girl.

MEIXIANG:

Yes, sir. Academician Wen is here.

MRS. LIU:

Ask him to come in.

MEIXIANG:

Please come in, sir.
(Wen greets Mistress Liu.)

MRS. LIU:

You have come very early today.

WEN:

As you asked me to teach the young lady music and calligraphy, I did not go to my office today.

MRS. LIU:

So you have set aside your public business for our sake! How very good you are to us! Meixiang, call your young mistress at once—her tutor is here.

MEIXIANG:

Yes, ma'am. Mistress Qianying, you are wanted!

QIANYING:

I was in my room when I heard my mother call.
I must go to her. *(She curtseys to her mother.)*

MRS. LIU:

Pay your respects to your cousin, child. From today on, he is your tutor.

QIANYING:

Yes, mother. *(She curtseys to Wen.)*

WEN *(aside)*:

In this dress she looks even lovelier than yesterday—a goddess!
> Her lotus skirt is flecked with kingfisher blue,
> Her soft neck is white as jade;
> Fairer than Daji who caused a kingdom's fall,
> Or Xishi who ruined a state,
> She is the angel who scatters lovesickness,
> And could I see this fair vision in my dreams
> I should not dread even the approach of dawn;
> The moon might sink and the lamp burn low,
> But I should sleep on till the sun
> Shone through my eastern window.
> Bring a lyre, and let the young lady play.
> Beside embroidered silk curtains
> In the gilded chamber,
> By screens inlaid with silver,
> What delight to listen to the seven strings
> As they echo joy and sorrow!
> This stately, unearthly music
> Sweeps away all worldly thoughts
> And banishes mundane cares;
> Her touch is light, and the music
> Is like the cry of wild storks in northern lands.

> *Resonance ripples from the golden stop-key,*
> *Sweet harmonies from the chilly strings,*
> *And the touch of her slender fingers is exquisite*
> *In this art she has mastered superbly.*
> *Most subtle in perception,*
> *Pretty as cherry blossom,*
> *Pure as the orchid,*
> *She embodies the rarest virtues*
> *Of earth and heaven!*

MRS. LIU:

Play that again. Then your tutor can point out any mistakes you still make.

WEN:

> *Skin white as snow,*
> *Hands like fade*
> *And fingernails like crystal,*
> *She sits with charm and distinction,*
> *Grace in her every movement,*
> *And her fade bracelets tinkle*
> *Before her gilded sleeves flutter.*

MRS. LIU:

That's enough of the lyre, child. Now prepare the incense, and let your cousin sit on your father's couch while you pay your respects. For since he is your tutor you must treat him as your father. Now, nephew, will you help her with her writing? *(Qianying writes.)*

WEN:

Keep your wrist down and your pen straight. No, not like that. *(He shows her how to hold the pen, and squeezes her hand.)*

QIANYING:

Where are your manners? How dare you hold my hand?

WEN:

I meant no harm.

MRS. LIU:
    You should think yourself very lucky, child, to have your cousin take your hand.

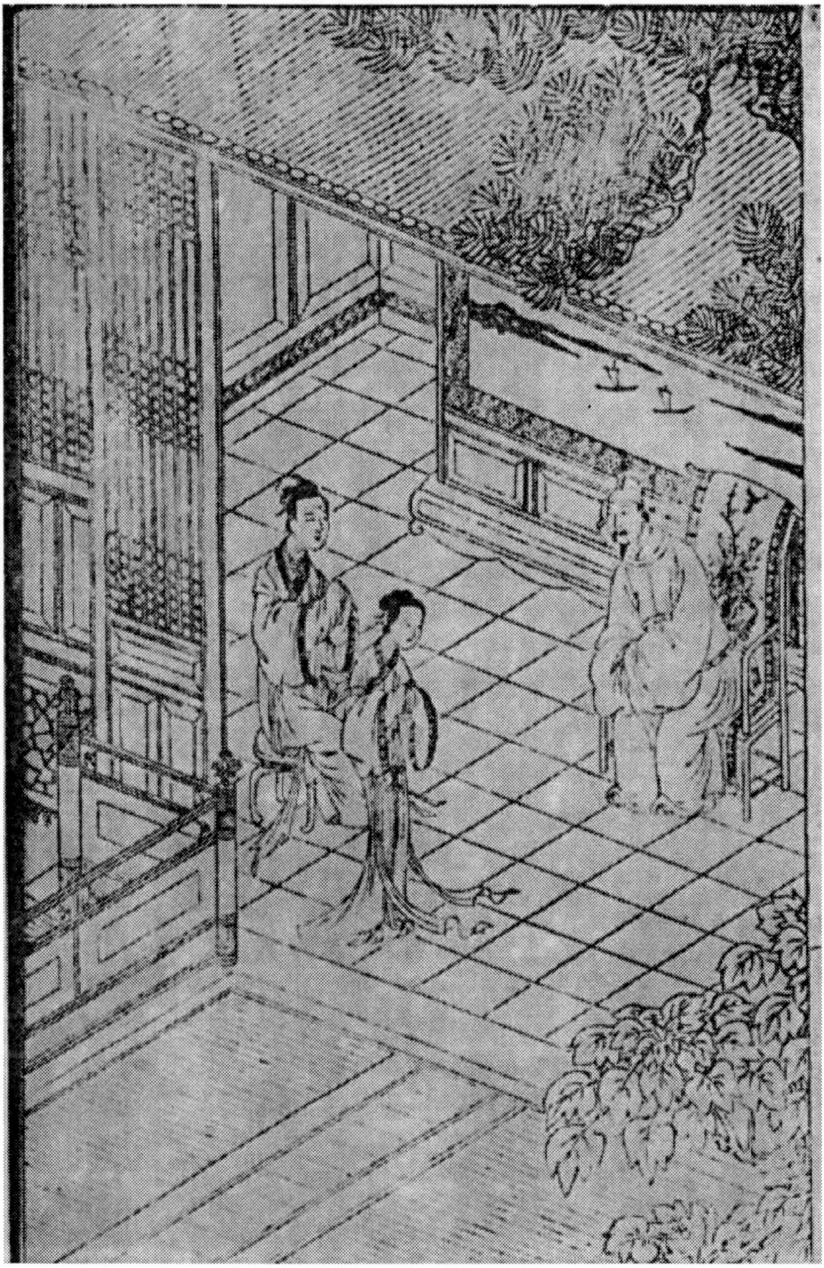

QIANYING:

"After the age of seven, boys and girls should not share one seat."[26]

MRS. LIU:

Now you're showing off your book-learning to your cousin.

WEN:

A gentle girl may appear stubborn at first;
I hope she is just being coy.
I congratulate myself on my good fortune—
What happiness to touch those tapering fingers!
How sweetly she flashed back at me!
However long she complains
I shall put up with it gladly.
This is better than being refuted
By the academy scholars!

No, that is not right. Keep your wrist down and your pen straight.

QIANYING *(angrily):*

There you go again!

WEN:

Oh, lucky brush
Of rabbit's hair and bamboo,
Caressed by such tender fingers!
Do keep down your slender wrist!
Her eyes flash again as I touch her,
Reproaching me for playing such a trick on her.

MRS. LIU:

Take your leave of your cousin now, child, and go back to your room.

---

[26] A quotation from the *Book of Rites*.

QIANYING:

    Yes, mother. *(She curtseys and goes out.)*

WEN:

    Excuse me for a moment, aunty. *(He walks after Qianying.)* I saw her walk down the steps and go this way, but all I noticed was her face and figure—not her feet. She has left footprints in the sand. How lucky that I followed her so quickly! Had I waited, a breeze might have blown these prints away, and I should not have seen how utterly perfect she is.

    Most slippers hide some lack of symmetry,
    The candid sand shows no mercy;
    But her footprints are flawless—
    Slender, well-formed and bewitching.
    She is charming in a passion,
    When she stamps her feet in anger.

    Now she has gone. When shall I see her again? How can I forget her?

    Tea will sober a drunkard,
    But I am intoxicated
    By her white teeth and bright eyes.
    I rack my brains for a good plan to win her,
    But my old aunt is watchful.
    I need no warning: this will be as hard
    As drawing water from a deep, deep well,
    Or catching gorillas with wine;
    But love deadens me to shame;
    I am willing to risk my life,
    With cunning deep as the ocean,
    Daring great as the sky.
    Flowers fall short of her charm,
    Willows of her slender waist,
    And her tiny feet are like the golden lotus.
    How could Heaven conceive such beauty,
    Matchless in the world of men?
    (He turns back)

MRS. LIU:

Excuse me, nephew, I would like to ask you a favour. My daughter has turned eighteen, but she isn't engaged yet. Your academy is full of fine scholars. Will you find a good match for her?

WEN *(aside):*

I must play a trick if I want to have my way. *(To Mistress Liu.)* I know a scholar there, aunty, no less gifted and learned than I am.

MRS. LIU:

Few scholars are your equal, I'll be bound. How old is this gentleman? What does he look like?

WEN:

He is my age, my build,
But a better scholar,
A bolder, more dashing man.
Take my word for it,
They will make a well-matched pair; (Aside.)
You do not know
That he is here before you!
Though the custom is to wed with ceremony,
If both sides are sincere
You need no extravagant dowry. (Aside)
Light lamps and spread the feast,
Then for a dreamless sleep in fairyland!
A fade mirror-stand shall be the betrothal gift.
A tussle lies ahead
By crimson candles on a moonlit night;
And I foresee
That my work is cut out for me!

After I have spoken to him and arranged a date for the marriage, I shall bring him here.

MRS. LIU:

It is very good of you to help.

(Wen starts off, laughing to himself.)

WEN:

Now, Wen Jiao, your greatest wish will come true. *(He goes out, to return very shortly with something in his hand!)*

Aunty, I have spoken to that scholar. Today is an auspicious day, and this jade mirror-stand is his betrothal gift. He will send a matchmaker to arrange the affair, but asked me to thank his future mother-in-law for him first.

Her sweet cheeks, snowy arms and downy neck
Shall be scented, powdered and tinted with cinnabar;
In spring we shall climb pagodas,
Walk arm in arm along winding corridors,
And search for new beauty spots.
In summer we shall haunt cool courts and pavilions,
Or rest by the immaculate green gauze window,
Threading pearls or catching glowworms with our fans.
In autumn when the frosty sky is clear
We will rest by painted screens
In halls fragrant with orchids;
We shall watch the stars of love
And burn incense to the moon.
In winter we shall pluck plum blossom
To set in antique vases,
And seek other pleasures too.
Then her slightest wish shall be law,
She may smile or frown,
For in every mood she is lovely.
I shall feast my eyes on her day and night,
Forgetting hunger, cold and all else beside. (Exit.)

MRS. LIU:

He has gone. Watch the gate, Meixiang, and tell me if anyone comes. *(Enter the Matchmaker!)*

MATCHMAKER:

Introducing couples is my job,
Making matches is my trade.

I am a matchmaker. Academician Wen has sent me to Mrs. Liu's house to fix a lucky day for his wedding. Here I am. As there's no one to announce me, I'll go straight in. *(She greets Mistress Liu.)* My respects, ma'am!

MRS. LIU:

Who sent you here?

MATCHMAKER:

The academician sent me to you to arrange the day for the young lady's marriage.

MRS. LIU:

Which academician?

MATCHMAKER:

Academician Wen.

MRS. LIU:

But he is the guarantor.

MATCHMAKER:

No, no! Not the guarantor, but your future son-in-law.

MRS. LIU:

What betrothal gift did he give?

MATCHMAKER:

The jade mirror-stand was his gift.

MRS. LIU:

The wretch! I'll smash it to pieces!

MATCHMAKER:

Stop! That mirror-stand was a present from the emperor. To break it would be most disrespectful, and the consequences might be very serious.

MRS. LIU:

Well! So he has deceived me. Meixiang, tell your young mistress to get ready. When we have fixed on a lucky day, we shall send her to her husband's house. Now I must go to the back. *(Exeunt)*

ACT III

(Enter Wen and Qianying escorted by the Matchmaker. Music sounds.)

WEN:

> *Now drums and flutes are played;*
> *If the girl won't have me,*
> *Then I must take her by force.*
> *Prepared for an awkward scene,*
> *I put on a bold front;*
> *If she frowns I shall plead with her*
> *Before the ivory couch.* (To the Matchmaker.)
> Stand in front of me, ma'am, while I have a look at her.

MATCHMAKER:

> All right. Now you can peep.
> *(Wen gazes at the girl.)*

QIANYING:

> What a boor!

WEN:

> *She is fuming with rage,*
> *She will not submit to me.*
> *As a poet I won preferment,*
> *Passed first in the imperial examinations,*
> *And at court wear official robes;*
> *But tonight I shall have my face scratched by my bride.*
> *I must screw up my courage and go up to her.*
> *Enough of these fears,*
> *I'll ignore the matchmaker*
> *And stay close by my bride.*
> *Why stand on ceremony'?*
> *I must step forward*
> *Even if she makes a scene.*

QIANYING:

If that fellow comes near me, I'll scratch his face! Make him go away! Come here, ma'am. I've something to tell you. When this fellow first turned up, my mother told me to pay my respects to him, and he accepted my curtsey.

MATCHMAKER:

Sir, the bride says that when she first met you she paid her respects to you, and you accepted her curtsey.

WEN:

I did not accept. Tell her that.

MATCHMAKER:

He says he did not accept, ma'am.

QIANYING:

He sat on my father's silver-inlaid armchair and accepted my curtsey.

MATCHMAKER:

She says you sat on her father's silver-inlaid armchair and accepted her curtsey.

WEN:

The sight of her sweet face
Would not let me sit unmoved;
I kicked aside the chair
And stood beside it.

QIANYING:

Come here, ma'am. He let me pay my respects to him another time too.

MATCHMAKER:

Sir, she says you let her pay her respects to you another time too.

WEN:

Never!

MATCHMAKER:

He says never, ma'am.

QIANYING:

When my mother told me to play the lyre and practise my calligraphy, he sat on my father's couch while I bowed to him as his pupil.

MATCHMAKER:

Sir, she says that before playing the lyre and practising calligraphy she bowed to you as her teacher, and seated on her father's couch, you accepted her bow.

WEN:

I simply sat on the edge of the couch,
And accepted two bows from her.
Now I bow back to you,
Returning your curtsey.
You have received what is your due,
And if I am honoured and pleased
That is my good luck.

QIANYING:

Tell him this! I am going to bed, and I don't want him to come near me. If he does, I shall scratch his ugly face so that he won't dare show it to anyone.

MATCHMAKER:

Sir, your bride says she is going to bed, and you must keep away. If you go near her, she will scratch your face so that you won't dare show it to anyone.

WEN:

My wife will sleep in the inner room
And I in the study, all alone as before.

> *But though I may never share her bed,*
> *When it is said that Wen Jiao has married Qianying,*
> *I shall still take pride in this!* Bring wine. Let me pour a cup for her. *(He pours out some wine.)*

QIANYING:
> I won't drink it.

MATCHMAKER:
> Take one cup, ma'am.

WEN:
> *When I first saw her in the stately hall*
> *I thought I was in heaven,*
> *And dared steal glances only,*
> *Not look her in the face.*
> *Now I can wait on her,*
> *I'd gladly be her slave.*
> *My larder holds rare dainties,*
> *My chests are crammed with silks and embroideries!*
> *If I can put on your trinkets*
> *And wait on you hand and foot,*
> *I shall be in paradise.*

QIANYING *(spilling the wine):*
> I won't drink!

WEN:
> *This is nothing.*
> *I filled the gold cup too full,*
> *So my court robe is wet;*
> *But a little stain is of no account;*
> *I can go and change my dress.*
> *I do not mind if whole casks of wine are spilt*
> *Or a hundred court robes stained,*
> *If my lady will relent.*
> *Tonight I know her plan,*
> *My sleeve is wet with wine—*

When will flowers deck my cap?

MATCHMAKER:

If the young lady goes on scorning her husband like this, she will be disobeying His Majesty's decree.

WEN:

Don't say such things, ma'am!
Don't talk of imperial decrees;
That will only enrage her more.
Beg her not to tarry,
Not to hesitate,
For the time is slipping away;
But if you speak of high position
Or of authority,
It will sound as if I am putting pressure on her.

But I beg you, ma'am, to help me! *(He kneels to the Matchmaker)*

MATCHMAKER:

Why do you kneel to me, sir?

WEN:

To ask the tail
Serves better than asking the head.
I bow to the matchmaker
To ask her to reason gently with my bride,
So that husband and wife can live in happiness.
This is a time when a third party is needed.

MATCHMAKER:

It is dawn now, sir, and you must go to your office. I shall report this to the old lady.

WEN:

I know what is in your heart, my dear, but listen to me—
You are young and want to marry a handsome youth,
Yet what is there in a few years?
I shall always know that you are too good for me;

You may be difficult to please,
But I shall always obey you.
You may sulk, but I shall beam;
You may be angry and swear at me,
But I shall still be happy,
For I look on you as my goddess and guiding star.
Just consider my position.
As my young and pretty wife,
You will not use your needle
Except to show your skill by stringing pearls;
You will not wet your hands
Except to wash them in warm, scented water.
Married to a minister,
You will have all the food and clothes you need;
I have carriage, horses and drivers ready for you;
Your equipage is handsomely turned out
With green tassels, gilded axle, silver nails,
And brightly painted wheels,
And no one else will share
Your smart, distinguished carriage.
If you marry some young noble,
Dishonest and full of deceit,
He will go riding all day;
At night he and his wife are lovebirds together,
But at dawn the husband flies;
He considers her a toy,
Treats her as rubbish to be tossed aside.
You may knit your brows through the night,
And turn to listen to the horses neighing
When loneliness keeps you from sleep.
The lamp grows dim but still he does not come
The incense burns away—no sign of him!
So in a few short years you pine away,
While he enjoys himself with concubines.
But I shall be true to you:
I shall not lay hands on the maids,
And even if fairies came down from the moon

I should not look at them.
Being slightly your senior
Makes me afraid of you—
That is how I know your thoughts.
So do not hanker after other men:
If you took a younger husband,
He would not treat you so well. (Exeunt!)

ACT IV

(Enter Prefect Wang with Attendants!)

PREFECT:

In this lofty capital
With dragon and phoenix pavilions,
A new sanded avenue
Is built for the minister.
But do not envy
My high estate and splendour;
Ten years ago
I was still a mere civilian.

I am Prefect Wang. Trouble has arisen over Academician Wen's marriage. I have invited Wen and his wife to a special feast at which I shall try to reconcile them. I shall put my plan into action when they arrive. They should be here now. *(Enter Wen and Qianying.)*

WEN:

Today the prefect has asked us to a feast. I do not know what he means by this, but we are going to see.

When husband and wife are estranged,
A third party's help is needed.
Today the prefect asks us both to a feast;
I ride my charger in front,
She sits in the carriage behind;
They say this country couple
Is as close as the fish to the water;
Man and wife refuse to be parted.
When Sima Xiangru sold wine
He had a young wife by the name of Zhuo;
But I had to go on my knees to mine,
For she was disgusted by her white-haired husband
And would not go quietly with me.
I write listlessly on the bridge
With none to complain to.
This is love's sweet sorrow which I brought on myself.

Here we are. *(To the Attendants.)* Go and announce that Academician Wen and his wife have arrived.

ATTENDANT:

Yes, sir. *(Announcing.)* Academician Wen and his wife are here.

PREFECT:

Ask them to come in.
(They greet each other.)

PREFECT:

By His Majesty's order I have prepared this feast to ask you to write a poem. If your poem is good, you shall drink wine from a gold goblet and your lady shall put a gold-phoenix pin in her hair and powder on her face. If your poem is bad, you shall drink water from an earthenware pitcher and your lady shall put straw in her hair and paint her face black.

QIANYING:

Do you hear that, sir? His Excellency says if you write a good poem, you will have wine. If you don't write a good one, you will have to drink cold water. Do take care!

WEN:

> *I have not written a couplet*
> *Since I passed the examinations,*
> *And after drinking all last night with friends*
> *Today my throat is parched—*
> *I would like a drink of water to quench my thirst.*
> *Well-water from an earthenware pot*
> *Will cool the passions, damp down noxious fumes,*
> *And counteract any poison.*
> *Water is a wonderful drink;*
> *You can cure a boil or swollen face*
> *With water and an incantation.*

PREFECT:

If there is no poem, the academician must drink water and the lady must paint her face with ink.

WEN:

The prefect must wait:
I need a draught to cool the passions first;
My lady is charmingly gowned,
Beautifully painted and powdered,
Fairer than a river nymph—
And she thinks herself more than a match for me.

QIANYING:

Do apply your mind to your poem, sir! If you don't write one, you will have to drink water and my face will be painted black—that would be too bad!

WEN:

You should address me as "husband," not as "sir."

QIANYING:

Very well, I'll call you "husband." Do concentrate, husband!

WEN:

You plague your husband in private,
But you cannot disobey the emperor's order—
There is something at least to control you.
It has taken you two months to call me "husband."
I have not yet enjoyed you,
Not yet touched your skin;
But when you call me "husband,"
You throw me into raptures!

QIANYING:

Husband! Do concentrate! Otherwise you will be punished with water; and if my face is painted black, what shall I do?

WEN:

> *Even if your face is painted,*
> *It will not be black for long;*
> *We have freshly-made, fragrant soap—*
> *Once home again you can wash in a silver basin.*

QIANYING:

Husband, do give your attention to your poem!

WEN:

> *I have never been much of a poet,*
> *What verses can I write*
> *Now that I am old and dull-witted?*
> *Today I am acting a part;*
> *Her alarm is rather touching,*
> *But I shall leave her in suspense*
> *Before I start to write.*

PREFECT:

Please write your poem, sir.

WEN:

Very well.

QIANYING:

Husband, do give your mind to it!

WEN:

> There is no cause for alarm, ma'am.
> *You should understand that*
> *Wen Jiao is no common scholar,*
> *But has read a great many books.*
> *Yet my learning won me no beauty,*
> *For you treated me with such disdain*
> *That I longed to sink through the earth.*
> *But though young men are easy to find,*
> *If a youth has to drink cold water*
> *And your face is painted black,*

What use are his handsome looks?

QIANYING:

Please, husband, write that poem! I don't want you to drink cold water.

WEN:

If I write a good poem, my dear, will you be kind to me?

QIANYING:

If you write a good poem, and I can wear a gold pin and drink the emperor's wine, then I promise to love you.

WEN:

In that case, my dear, you need not worry.
I take paper and ink; my brush is ready at hand;
I shall drink from the silver cup.
A glance, at the pitcher of water does not dismay me—
It will sober me after drinking.
I am not in the least alarmed.
My knowledge is all-embracing as rivers and lakes,
But my wife despises my scholarship
And considers me as useless;
She has tormented me so
That I will pose as befuddled.
Now she moves forward, a suppliant...
But I pay no attention to her.
She is all meekness now,
A shrew no more! (He chants his poem)
When the academician sits down in the hall.
And composes a verse, he dumbfounds one and all;
He has won royal wine and renown by his pen,
For the emperor honours all talented men.

PREFECT:

You certainly have genius, sir, to throw off such an excellent poem. Let his lady put on the gold hairpin and drink the royal wine.

QIANYING *(delighted):*

    I thank you with all my heart, sir!

WEN:

    You seem rather pleased with me now, ma'am.

PREFECT:

    Are you willing to be his wife now, ma'am?

QIANYING:

    Yes, I am willing.

PREFECT:

    In that case I shall prepare another feast to congratulate you both.

WEN:

> *You fear the strong and torment the weak,*
> *But now you must repay my love*
> *And repent of what you did.*
> *With this poem I made you love me.*
> *This is like the famous reply to the foreign envoy—*
> *Each word completely correct.*[27]
> *She has a gold pin in her hair,*
> *I drink from the gold goblet,*
> *And we will carry many gifts away.*
> *No more will the lovely bride*
> *Despise her elderly husband.*

PREFECT:

    There is no happier occasion than a reconciliation between a husband and wife. We shall kill sheep and prepare wine for a congratulatory feast.

---

[27] There is a legend that when a certain foreign envoy came to the Tang court, Li Bai, the great poet, was the only one able to understand his language and write a reply.

We feast with gold goblets brimming with wine;
Fluting and singing accompany the banquet;
Today their joy is complete;
The distinguished husband and wife will ever.
(Wen bows to the Prefect)

WEN:

I thank you, sir, for your help.
Now our marriage is a true one,
The sorrows of love are ended,
We shall take delight in each other—
This is better than sleeping alone.
Sima Xiangru in his tavern
Would not give up Lady Zhuo.
From now on we shall live in harmony—
By my own exertions I have won my love.
(THE END)

LORD GUAN GOES TO THE FEAST

CHARACTERS
LU SU, *a minister of the Kingdom of Wu*
QIAO GONG, *a senior statesman*
SIMA HUI, *a wise hermit*
BOY
HUANG WEN, *a general of the Kingdom of Wu*
LORD GUAN, *a general of the Kingdom of Shu, Governor of Jingzhou*
his sons
GUAN PING
GUAN XING
ZHOU CANG, *Lord Guan's lieutenant*
ZANG GONG, *an officer of the Kingdom of Wu*
LU SU'S TROOPS
LORD GUAN'S TROOPS

ACT I

(Enter Lu Su, Huang Wen and Soldiers.)

LU:

Three feet of steel, ten thousand books—
For what am I destined by Heaven?
Statesmen of the east, generals of the west—
What were they?
I am the equal of them all. I am Lu Su, Minister to the King of Wu. My master, Sun Quan, rules over the Changjiang River Valley, while Cao Cao, King of Wei, holds the north, and Liu Bei, King of Shu, the west. Formerly we controlled the strategic province of Jingzhou, and by holding it securely kept the empire divided into three. But when Zhou Yu died at Jiangling I urged our king to let Liu Bei occupy Jingzhou for a time, so that we could join forces against Cao Cao. I acted as guarantor for that. Then our master gave his younger sister to Liu Bei. However, the scoundrel's friendship was false—he tricked us by seizing Yizhou, and annexed Hanzhong, hoping to set himself up as emperor. Now I want to take Jingzhou back, but Lord Guan who is governor there will certainly not return it. I have therefore sent General Huang Wen with a memorial to our king proposing three plans, in which I urge that since Lord Guan is so able, is determined to annex our territory, and holds the upper reaches of the river, we should demand the return of Jingzhou, so that we may control the whole Chang-jiang River Valley. My plans are: First, since the kings of both our states are related by marriage, we can prepare a feast with music by the Changjiang River, and write to congratulate Lord Guan on Liu Bei's recent victory over Cao Cao, the establishment of his rule in Hanzhong, and the great achievements of the Kingdom of Shu. We will invite Lord Guan to cross the river to our feast, and he will hardly suspect us. Should he come, during the banquet we will ask him courteously for the return of Jingzhou. If he agrees, well and good. If not, we can carry out our second plan—seize all his ships and detain him. Once this is done and he knows he is caught in a trap, he should think better of it and return

us our province. If he still refuses, we can resort to our third plan—conceal armed men behind the arras, and signal to them during the drinking to come out and take him captive. Lord Guan is Liu Bei's right hand. We shall let him go back to Yizhou only after he agrees to return us Jingzhou. In any case, the commander's absence will throw his troops into disorder, and by seizing this opportunity we should have no difficulty in recapturing Jingzhou in one battle. These are the three plans which I gave to Huang Wen. I have asked Qiao Gong here to discuss them.

古杭新刊的本關大王單刀會

駕一行上開住　外末上奏住云　駕云　外末云住
正末扮喬國老上　住　外末云　尋思云　今日三分已
安忽引干戈又交生靈受苦您眾宰相每也合諫天子响
過去見禮數了　駕云　陛下万歳〻　奂微臣愚見那
荆州不可取　駕又云　不可去〻〻

【點絳唇】咱本文嘗國目僚坎為他坡君欽弱吳恐鬧當日五
処鎗刀併了童卓誅了衣紹存的孫刘曹揭平分
一國作三朝不付と河淸海晏而順民調兵器改為農器用征
旗不動酒旌搖軍罷戰馬添原余气散陣雲消役將校作旦僚
脫金甲石羅袍恨削旗捲虎潛竿股間劒挿龍歸鞘拱治的民
安國泰却又早將老兵喬　駕云　啞合與它浪上九州恕
當日曹操本來取　　吳生被那弟兄每當住　駕末云住

(Enter Qiao Gong.)

QIAO:

I am Qiao Gong. Now the empire is divided into three, with Cao Cao in the north, Sun Quan in the Changjiang River Valley and Liu Bei in the west. Before Liu Bei scored such successes, our king gave him the use of Jingzhou as a base, but he has not yet returned it. Though Lu Su has determined to win it back, he has not yet taken any action. Today he has sent for me. I must go and see what he wants. Who could have foreseen this break-up of the Han Empire?

I was a subject of Han,
But the emperor was a weakling,
Discontent was rife,
And five rebellions broke out.
Two warlords were killed, leaving only
Sun Quan, Liu Bei and Cao Cao,
Who divided one state into three.
Now the world is at peace again,
The wind and waves are calmed
And the rain propitious;
Swords are turned into ploughshares,
Martial banners are furled,
But signs hang from every tavern;
Fighting has ceased, horses grow sleek,
Hatred is at an end, the air is clear,
And generals turn into ministers,
Changing their gleaming armour for silken robes.
Here at headquarters flags remain furled,
Swords remain in their sheaths,
Our troops are strong, our horses mettlesome,
The officers grow old, the conscripts swagger. Now I have arrived. Report that Qiao Gong is here, man.

SOLDIER *(announcing him):*

Your Honour, Qiao Gong has come.

LU:

>Invite him in.

SOLDIER:

>His Honour asks you to go in.
>*(Qiao Gong greets Lu)*

QIAO:

>Your Honour sent for me. May I know your wishes?

LU:

>I asked you to come today, sir, to discuss the recovery of Jingzhou.

QIAO:

>You will never recapture Jingzhou. Lord Guan is as brave as a tiger. Even if you make such a request, he and his sworn brothers will certainly refuse you.

LU:

>Though he has many sworn brothers, his force is a small one.

QIAO:

>*You say he has many friends*
>*But not many troops.*
>Do you know, Your Honour, how he burned the camp at Bowang?

LU:

>No. I should like to hear, sir.

QIAO:

>*He hemmed the enemy general in.*
>And have you heard of his tactics in the river battle?

LU:

>I heard some talk of that. I should like to know more.

QIAO:

> Zhou Yu and Jiang Gan were old friends,
> Zhuge Liang made a crafty plan,
> Huang Gai had himself beaten
> And offered grain to the enemy[28]
> That was a fine battle at Red Cliff![29]

LU:

I have some recollection of it, but should like to hear the tale again.

QIAO:

> Snapped bows burned like dry reeds,
> Banners flared up like fuel,
> Drums rolled and then fell silent,
> Carved shields littered the field,
> Steeds smouldered in their harness,
> And corpses lay in their battle-dresses and helmets
> As Cao Cao's million were routed.
> Not a single man escaped—
> All perished by fire or water;
> Either burned in the flames
> Or drowned in the rushing river.
> Had not Heaven defended the just
> Our kingdom would have fallen to Cao Cao!

---

[28] Jiang Gan was a follower of Cao Cao. On Zhuge Liang's advice, Zhou Yu planted a letter casting suspicion on two of Cao Cao's generals where Jiang Gan was bound to find it. This made Cao Cao lose trust in these men. Then Huang Gai, one of Zhou Yu's generals, pretended to have been driven out by him and went over to Cao Cao, later betraying him.

[29] Cao Cao was persuaded by false friends to rope his boats together at Red Cliff. As soon as the wind was in the right direction, the enemy started a fire which destroyed his entire fleet.

LU:

Cao Cao is a mighty warrior and a shrewd one. He overthrew his rivals and seized the throne. He may imprison Liu Bei in Yongan Palace and hold both your daughters in the Tower of Bronze Sparrows.

QIAO:

Even if my daughters are captive
We are allies now,
And one false move
Would cause irreparable harm.

LU:

We have a million fine troops here and a thousand officers. What can he do to us?

QIAO:

Do you mean to use brute force?
To provoke a war?

LU:

Lord Guan is growing old. He has more courage than ability.

QIAO:

You will not get the better of him,
Though he is old.

Let me tell you how General Zhou Yu went to collect grain in Sichuan.

LU:

I have not heard that. Go on.

QIAO:

Collecting grain in the west,
Zhou Yu lost his life;
Zhang Fei by the River Han
Stopped the men bearing home his corpse,

> *And standing in the prow*
> *You nearly fell over with fright—*
> *Yet you want to recover Jingzhou!*
> *When Lord Guan knows of this*
> *He will rain down blows like hailstones.*

LU:

What can he do?

QIAO:

> *He killed one general in a fit of rage,*
> *Another to show his skill;*
> *Galloping through a million men,*
> *He strikes off enemy heads as if in sport.*

LU:

Speaking of the battle of the Red Cliff, Liu Bei ought to be grateful to us.

QIAO:

> *You were outwardly on good terms,*
> *But his smile hid daggers.*

LU:

If he gives me back Jingzhou, well and good. If not, I shall take it by storm.

QIAO:

> *If you unleash a war,*
> *You cannot blame Heaven for the calamity*
> *When you brought it on yourself,*
> *By acting without any faith or kindness.*
> *And how do you compare with crafty Cao Cao*
> *Who is no match for the wily Zhuge Liang?*

LU:

If he will not return Jingzhou, I shall take it by force.

QIAO:
> *You will throw your troops into a bloody battle,*
> *Not caring if thousands are killed.*

LU:

I have never met this Lord Guan, sir. How good a soldier is he?

QIAO:

When Lord Guan rides into battle whirling his sword, ten thousand men cannot withstand him.
> *His tufted beard streams in the wind,*
> *With his huge frame he is a tiger,*
> *Or like a god among lesser deities.*
> *His enemies blench at the sight*
> *And take leave of their senses.*
> If you pit yourself against him—
> *Put on all your armour,*
> *All your battle-dresses;*
> *For even a million men*
> *Cannot check his galloping horse;*
> *Even a thousand generals*
> *Are no match for his scimitar.*

LU:

Let me tell you something, sir. I have three good plans for recovering Jingzhou.

QIAO:

What are they?

LU:

The first plan is this: since the kings of both our states are related by marriage, we can prepare a feast with music by the Changjiang River, and write to congratulate Lord Guan on Liu Bei's recent victory over Cao Cao, the establishment of his rule in Hanzhong, and the great achievements of the Kingdom of Shu. We will invite Lord Quan to cross the river to our feast, and he will hardly suspect us. Should he come, during the banquet we will ask him courteously for the return of Jingzhou. If he agrees, well and good. If not, we can carry out our second plan—seize all his ships and detain him. Once this is done and he knows he is caught in a trap, he should think better of it and return us our province. If he still refuses, we can resort to our third plan—conceal armed men behind the arras, and signal to them during the drinking to come out and take him captive. Lord Guan is Liu Bei's right hand. We shall let him go back to Yizhou only after he agrees to return us Jingzhou. In any case, the commander's absence will throw his troops into disorder, and by seizing this opportunity we should have no difficulty in recapturing Jingzhou in one battle. These are my three plans, which will leave him no way out.

QIAO:

>A thousand plans will not trap him, let alone three.
>*You say these three plans will outwit him,*
>*But bear in mind—*
>*If you offend Lord Guan,*
>*Your brave soldiers and crafty scholars*
>*Will be no match for him.*

LU:

>What sort of drinker is Lord Guan?

QIAO:

>*In his cups he shows his daring,*
>*He will suddenly grasp your jade belt*
>*And whirl his sword over your head.*

LU:

>I shall seize his warships at the shore.

QIAO:

>*You may seize his warships at the shore.*
>*But if he wants to go back—*
>*You will have to make a floating bridge for him.*

LU:

Stop trying to dissuade me, sir. I have my well-laid plans and the time has come—Jingzhou must be retaken.

QIAO:

Your Honour, how do you think your plans compare with the three Cao Cao made on Baling Bridge? You will end by falling into Lord Guan's hands.

LU:

I never heard that story. Please tell it me, sir.

QIAO:

Cao Cao was holding the stirrup-cup
And the parting gifts were ready;
His nephew and sisters-in-law were in a panic,
For he is full of cunning and acts with caution.
But Lord Guan, who was also a friend,
Came early to Baling Bridge,
Striking terror into all the generals there.
When he reined in his wind-swift steed
And swung his crescent-shaped sword,
Cao Cao, for all his plans,
Became a laughing-stock.

Lord Guan simply said: "Excuse me, Your Honour, if I do not alight."

And with the point of his sword
He picked up the silk battle-dress. (Exit.)

LU:

Qiao Gong has said a great deal about Lord Guan's might, but I find it hard to believe him, Huang Wen. By the river bank there lives another talented scholar, Sima Hui, who once knew Lord Guan. I shall invite him to a feast to question him about Lord Guan's courage and cunning and his temper after drinking. Come with me now to his hermitage to find him. *(Exeunt.)*

ACT II

(Enter Sima Hui with a Boy.)

SIMA:

I am Sima Hui. Now the Han Empire is divided into three kingdoms. Several years have passed since Liu Bei left me, and I have built a thatched cottage by the river, where I study the holy law. It is very peaceful here.

The proud angler for huge sea-monsters
Has become a simple ploughman;
Scorning Ying Bu, Peng Yue and Han Xin[30]
I keep my hands, which once reached for the stars,
Folded in hempen sleeves,
Gathering country folk
And rustic poets round me
To enjoy fresh fish and wine;
Drinking from a single cup
Of earthenware or porcelain,
We sing aloud and clap hands,
Not caring if the day be foul or fair;
When drunk I curl up in my quilt
And sleep till the sun comes shining through my low window.
I am prouder than any great noble,
Free to do as I please.

Boy, go and see who that is at the gate.

BOY:

Yes, master.
(Enter Lu Su.)

---

[30] Generals who helped the first emperor of the Han Dynasty to win his kingdom.

LU:

    Here we are. See to my horse. *(He catches sight of the Boy.)* Is your master in, lad?

BOY:

    He is.

LU:

    Go and tell him Lu Su has come to pay his respects.

BOY:

    Lousy, are you? I'll tell him. *(He goes up to Sima Hui.)* Master, me son.

SIMA:

    How dare you call me your son?

BOY:

    I didn't mean that. You are my master, I am your disciple, and a disciple is like a son. That's what I meant by "master, me son."

SIMA:

    Stop talking nonsense. Who is at the door?

BOY:

    Lu Su has come to pay his respects.

SIMA:

    Ask him in.

BOY:

    Very good. *(He goes out to Lu Su.)* Please come in.
(Lu Su greets Sima Hui.)

SIMA:

    Good day, Your Honour.

LU:

The press of worldly affairs has long prevented me from seeking your instructions.

SIMA:

Yes, we have not met for several years. What brings you here today?

LU:

I have come to invite you to a feast by the river.

SIMA:

I am living a hermit's life here. Out of touch as I am with all that goes on in the world, of what use can I be to you? Why should Your Honour trouble to prepare a feast?

I am not the fisherman Lu Shang at the Fan Stream;[31]
I should cut a sorry figure at a banquet,
For I live by hills and streams like Xu You of old.[32]

What other guests have you asked?

LU:

Only your old friend Guan Yu, Marquis of Shou-Ting. No one else.

SIMA:

My old friend, Marquis of Shou-Ting?
Oh, no! If Lord Guan is coming, I am ill. I cannot go.

LU:

First you accept my invitation, but when you hear Lord Guan will be there you decline. Why is this, sir? You have met Lord Guan. All I want you to do is to drink a cup with him.

---

[31] Lu Shang, who helped King Wen of Zhou to overthrow the Shangs.

[32] A hermit of the time of King Yao.

SIMA:
> *You want me to drink with him,*
> *But will he keep his temper?*

LU:

If you ask him to drink, he can hardly take it amiss.

SIMA:
> *It is no use preparing wine and meat,*
> *Once Lord Guan is in a rage, blood will be spilt.*
> *Will you risk your life for that province across the river?*
> *Shall I risk mine for a feast?*
> *No, Your Honour, the two of us*
> *Would end as headless corpses.*

LU:

But as a guest what have you to be afraid of?

SIMA:

> *As a guest I might share your misfortune.*

LU:

I have three plans for recovering Jingzhou.

SIMA:

> *You have three plans to achieve undying fame,*
> *But why should I risk my life for one cup of wine?*
> *The mere thought of it appalls me!*

LU:

As old friends, what harm is there in having a drink together?

SIMA:

I see you are set on asking him. Well, if you listen to me no harm will be done. If not, you had better not ask him.

LU:

Go on. I am listening.

SIMA:
>This is it. When Lord Guan alights from his horse—
>*Bow and greet him courteously.*
>Will you do that?

LU:
>When Lord Guan alights I should bow and greet him? Certainly, I agree.

SIMA:
>*On bent knees offer him wine,*
>*Let him eat and drink his fill,*
>*Go east or west as he wills,*
>*And, most important of all—*
>*The moment he is drunk*
>*We must slip away!*

LU:
>How does he behave after drinking, sir?

SIMA:
>*He is wild enough when sober,*
>*But full of fight after wine;*
>*You must keep a watch on your tongue,*
>*And not let the name of Jingzhou pass your lips.*

LU:
>What if I do?

SIMA:
>If you mention Jingzhou,
>*He will flash his phoenix eyes,*
>*Stretch out his death-dealing hands,*
>*And furrow his shaggy brows*
>*Like a mountain ablaze.*
>*If he stoops from his towering height*
>*Prepare to leave!*
>*If he draws his sword*

> *Be ready to lose your head!*
> *You will never recover Jingzhou.*

LU:

You need not worry, sir. Lord Guan may be brave, but I fancy he lacks cunning. When the time comes I shall hide armed men behind the arras to seize him. Then even if he has wings, he will not be able to fly across the river. The first to strike will win.

SIMA:

> You will not be able to touch him.
> *Before you can lay hands on him*
> *Zhuge Liang will report the matter*
> *To the good and great-hearted Liu Bet.*
> *Zhuge Liang with his lyre can bring snow,*
> *And his sword frightens ghosts and demons;*
> *You have no hope of succeeding.*

LU:

I do not share your high opinion of Zhuge Liang. And apart from him, Liu Bei has no mighty warriors.

SIMA:

Lord Guan has four sworn brothers. When they hear of this, they will not let you off lightly.

LU:

Who are they?

SIMA:

> *General Huang Zhong, fierce as a leopard;*
> *Zhao Yun, a tiger for courage;*
> *Ma Chao, that great slayer of men;*
> *And stout Zhang Fei, who at Hulao Pass*
> *Fought the barons single-handed;*
> *He rides on a coal-black charger*
> *With a lance more than ten feet long;*
> *When he thundered at Dangyang Slope,*
> *He scattered Cao Cao's million;*

*When he glared, a dust storm sprang up
And the bridge was shattered;
When he shouted, great waves reared high
And the river flowed backwards.
These men will not stay their hands.*

LU:

I beg you to come to my feast, sir. What does it matter if Lord Guan is there too?

SIMA:

No, no, Your Honour. And don't complain that I didn't warn you.
*The point of his sword may scratch your hand,
Leaves may fall and break my head.
When Lord Guan went out alone to find two comrades,
With one horse and sword he awed the entire land,
For he was like a tiger roaming the hills,
His horse was like a sea-monster wreaking havoc;
With raised blade he killed Che Zhou,
Then made an end of Wen Chou,
Struck off Yan Liang's head beneath his flag,
And slaughtered brave Cai Yang.
If I accept—I who want a quiet life—
Farewell!
Will that executioner spare me?
(Exit)*

BOY:

Lu Su, you are too dense to see my worth. If you want Jingzhou, why not ask me? Lord Guan is my boon companion. I'll get him to hand over Jingzhou.

LU:

Since your master will not go, boy, you had better come to my feast.

BOY:
Yes, I'll go down the hill and attend your feast. I'll tell him to hand the place back.
I shall go to different houses trailing my stick,
And wander everywhere in my hempen shoes.
If I go—
When I offend Lord Guan, that will be too bad!
Brother Zhou Gang will come after me
And his sword will split my skull!
Tucking my head in like a frightened tortoise,
I shall scuttle for safety into the River Bian. (Exit)

LU: I am beginning to be alarmed myself by all this talk. Still, with my three plans why should I be afraid? Huang Wen, take this invitation for me to Jingzhou to Lord Guan, then bring me his reply. Make all the speed you can. *(Exeunt.)*

ACT III

(Enter Lord Guan with his sons Guan Ping and Guan Xing and Zhou Cang.)

LORD:

I am Guan Yu, a native of Xieliang in Puzhou. I serve Liu Bei as his chief general. Since the empire split into three, Cao Cao has occupied the north, Sun Quan has occupied the land south of the Changjiang River, and my sworn brother Liu Bei has occupied Sichuan and ordered me to govern Jingzhou and defend it well. Many years ago, when the armies of Chu and Han contended together, Liu Bang in his goodness and justice relied on three able men—Xiao He, Han Xin and Zhang Liang—while Xiang Yu relied on his own courage and might. Xiang Yu the Conqueror could lift a huge cauldron or tear down a mountain boulder; yet after more than seventy battles, great and small, he was forced to take his own life at Wujiang. Then Liu Bang ascended the throne and the Han Dynasty was established. But now the country is in turmoil again.

The whole empire was in tumult
In the hands of Xiang Yu and Liu Bang,
And the first to enter Xianyang would win the day.
One had strength to tear down mountains,
One had generosity as deep as the sea.
The two of them started equal,
But Liu Bang reigned in state
While Xiang Yu died at Wujiang.
One relied on three able men,
One killed his eight lieutenants;
So one perished at his own hands,
The other ascended the throne in a hushed court
Generation after generation
The rule was handed down and homage paid,
Till Emperor Xian lost support,
Dong Zhuo was neither good nor just,
And rough Lu Bu ran wild.

When Zhang Fei, Liu Bei and I became sworn brothers in the peach orchard, we sacrificed a white horse to heaven and a black ox to the earth, and swore that though born on different days we would choose to die together.

Zhang Fei came from Fanyang,
Liu Bei from Lousang,
I myself from Puzhou,
And at Nanyang was Zhuge Liang;
So heroes arose on all sides,
And we became sworn brothers, Liu, Guan and Zhang.
Three times we climbed the Sleeping-Dragon Mount
To invite Zhuge Liang to join us,
And at last the empire was carved into three.
Liu Bei has no match as a monarch,
And alone I govern Jingzhou.
No end to the battles on the river,
Waves impelling each other on! Son, go to the door and see who is there.

GUAN PING:

Yes, father.
(Enter Huang Wen.)

HUANG:

I am Huang Wen. I have brought a letter to Jingzhou inviting Lord Guan to a feast. Now I have arrived. Guards, kindly announce that Lu Su from across the river has sent Huang Wen the Dauntless here with an invitation.

GUAN PING:

Wait here while I announce you. *(He goes in to Lord Guan.)* Father, Lu Su from across the river has sent a general here with an invitation.

LORD:

Let him come in.

GUAN PING:

Come in.
(Huang Wen greets Lord Guan)

LORD:

Who is this fellow?

HUANG *(nervously):*

I am Huang Wen. Lu Su from across the river sent me here with an invitation. Here it is.

LORD:

You may go back first. I shall be coming soon.

HUANG:

I see Lord Guan looks as brave as a god. I tremble for you, Lu Su!
I, General Huang Wen,
Have come to invite Lord Guan.
His beard is two feet long,
His face is crimson,
His gleaming scimitar
Weighs eighty pounds;
If once that touches my neck—
Goodbye to Huang Wen!
If he comes, we shall feast;
If not, I may drink alone. (Exit.)

LORD:

Son, Lu Su has asked me to a feast. I mean to go.

GUAN PING:

That will not be a friendly feast, father. You had better not go.

LORD:

That does not matter.
The river divides our two kingdoms,

And now Lu Su has invited me to a feast.
This is no common banquet,
No gay affair in a painted hall
With foaming wine in phoenix cups—
No, he is preparing arsenic and hemlock;
And instead of girls, painted and powdered,
There will be pitiless warriors.
He wants to entrap the dragon
By spreading cunning snares;
This is no entertainment;
But a gory field of war.
Do not speak of honour and integrity,
He cares nothing for the verdict of posterity;
But since he has invited me,
I must go.

GUAN PING:

That fellow Lu Su is a clever, crafty man, with many troops and officers—good fighters with sturdy steeds. If you go, I am afraid you may be trapped.

LORD:

What if he has many officers, men and good horses?
When a hero marches forward and braves death,
Even ten thousand foes cannot stand against him.

GUAN PING:

The river is so wide, how are my men to come to your rescue?

LORD:

You think when the battle rages across the river
You will not be able to reach me;
But I shall get that rogue to escort me back,
Bowing as I go aboard.

GUAN PING:

I mean to cross the river with horsemen and warships, carving out a way with my sword. It is better to strike the first blow.

LORD:

*So you think the first to strike will win
While the one who delays will be lost?
But I shall seize his belt,
And boldly draw my bright sword.*

GUAN PING:

But what if he has laid an ambush, father?

LORD:

*He may have laid an ambush in the dark,
But I know how to take precautions.*
They are merely foxes and jackals! Why shouldn't I go to his feast?
*I have travelled hundreds of miles alone,
And killed generals at five passes.*
Let us see what he can do, son.

GUAN PING:

I never heard how you escaped from Xuchang. Will you tell me the story, father?

LORD:

*That was no more than when
I took my nephew to Yuan Shao,
Or Liu Bei's wife to him;
Fearless on Baling Bridge,
On my well-made saddle,
Before the drum rolled three times
I killed Cai Yang.*
After shedding blood in battle,
Catching up the gift robe with my sword
I left Xuchang,

Striking terror into Cao Cao.
Now I am going to the banquet alone,
To face their ministers and warriors—
This is no more than that banquet at Xiangyang.

GUAN PING:

They have a great force ready, father.

LORD:

What if they have?
They may have fierce troops
Stationed ready at their camp,
But my strategy is superior.
With a marvellous horse,
Invulnerable as a god—
Not that I am unduly confident—
At talk of battle my hands begin to itch!
Make ready spears, armour and banners;
Prepare for the fight!
I am Lord Guan, champion of the three kingdoms,
And my valour knows no bounds! Prepare a boat, son.
I shall take Zhou Cang to the banquet.

GUAN PING:

Take good care of yourself, father!

LORD:

This is not like the meeting with Duke Mu at Lingdong[33]
Nor the meeting with Xiang Yu at Hongmen;[34]
What if their foremost generals attend the feast?
I killed Yan Liang amid a million men. (Exit.)

---

[33] Duke Mu of the State of Qin met the King of Chu at Lingdong, meaning to capture him.

[34] Xiang Yu invited Liu Bang to a banquet at Hongmen, meaning to kill him; but Liu Bang escaped.

ZHOU:

Lord Guan has left for the feast. I had better go too.
My brave spirit aspires to the skies,
Today I shall show my prowess;
Let all prepare bows and arrows,
Put on armour and battle-dress;
Flags shall wave like writhing dragons,
As our men display their courage in the fight;
Though Lu Su has a thousand plans,
He will be no match for Lord Guan! Well, I am off to the banquet. *(Exit)*

GUAN XING:

Father has gone to the feast, brother. Let us go to his aid. Follow me, men!
Let embroidered banners flutter,
And painted drums sound the charge;
Let lances and swords surge forward like a river,
And troops charge swift as the wind,
Till unhappy corpses cover the whole plain
And, torn apart, the sons and fathers weep.
Then with gay whips beating our gilded stirrups,
Laughing and singing, we shall ride back in triumph.
(Exit.)

GUAN PING:

Both my father and brother have gone. I must follow to help them. Listen to my orders, men. Rein in your steeds, muffle your drums. There is to be no whispering, talking or din. Keep your bows and arrows ready and your swords unsheathed. We must all acquit ourselves like men.
Sabres and two-edged swords
Will whirl like swans in flight,
Tridents and maces will glitter in the sun;
Banners and lances will obscure the sky,
Crossbows and clubs will smash our enemy's skulls,
While ropes and red cotton halters fly overhead—

So we battle to show our might!
Now with a mighty force I cross the river,
A forest of swords and spears on either bank.
Our sailors do not fear the tossing waves,
Our soldiers do not fear the iron-clad foe;
Lord Guan will fight his way into the feast,
And show what a hero is made of.
Alone on horseback he will smite Lu Su
As he once killed Yan Liang.

Come with me, men, to your commander's assistance!

(Exit.)

ACT IV

(Enter Lu Su.)

LU:

There can be no day as happy as today. I am Lu Su. I dispatched Huang Wen with an invitation to Lord Guan, who consented readily to come to the feast today. So Jingzhou will be ours again! My brave armed men are hidden behind the arras. I have sent scouts to watch the river. When his boat comes, they will report to me. *(Enter Lord Guan and Zhou Cang.)*

LORD:

Where are we now, Zhou Cang?

ZHOU:

We are in the middle of the stream.

LORD:

This great river is a noble sight!
A thousand billows flow eastwards,
A few dozen rowers are with me in this small craft;
I go to no nine-storeyed dragon-and-phoenix palace,
But a lair, ten thousand feet deep, of tigers and wolves.
A stout fellow is never afraid,
I go to this feast as if to a country fair.
What a magnificent river!
Tossing waves, hill after hill—
Where is young Zhou Yu today?
He has turned to dust.
General Huang Gai suffered much;
The warships that conquered Cao Cao are no more,
But the waves are still warm from past battles—
This wrings my heart! This is no river water,
But the blood of heroes
Shed for these twenty years!
Here we are. Announce my arrival.
(An Attendant announces Lord Guan.) (Lu Su greets him.)

LU:

    This is simply a small gathering by the river. Our wine is no elixir, and our music just the poor tunes of this dusty world. It was good of Your Lordship to condescend to come.

LORD:

    I have done nothing to deserve this honour. Of course I was glad to come.

LU:

    Bring wine, Huang Wen. Let me offer Your Lordship a cup.

LORD:

    Your health, Your Honour! *(They drink.)* When you think back, the time has passed very quickly.

LU:

    Yes, indeed. The years gallop by like swift horses, and worldly affairs pass like fallen flowers or the water of a flowing stream.

LORD:

> *Think of the heroes of old—*
> *Where are King Shun's five ministers*
> *Or the three able men of Han?*
> *Living in two different kingdoms,*
> *We have not met for many years;*
> *Now face to face again,*
> *We are both growing old.*
> *Let us drink to our hearts' content,* More wine!
> *Let us drink our fill this night. (They drink.)*

LORD:

    Both the just and the unjust, you know, should be requited.

LU:

Since you mention it, I think it unjust to borrow without returning. Your Lordship is well versed in the arts of peace and war; you have mastered the books of military strategy, as well as the history of the Spring and Autumn Period.[35] You have aided those in distress and defended the state—this shows your humanity. You treat Liu Bei as your brother, and Cao Cao as your enemy—this shows your sense of justice. You left Cao Cao for Liu Bei, giving up high office and gold—this shows your probity. You vanquished Yu Jin without a fight, simply by drowning his army—this shows your wisdom. The only pity is that you break your word, so you lack one of the five virtues. If only you kept faith, no one could compare with Your Lordship.

LORD:

How do I break my word?

LU:

It is not your fault—your brother Liu Bei is faithless.

LORD:

In what way?

LU:

When Liu Bei was defeated at Dangyang and had nowhere to turn, I arranged for him to station his troops at Xiakou and elsewhere. Then I went with Zhuge Liang to our sovereign, and we lost no time in mobilizing our troops and defeating Cao Cao at Red Cliff. The expedition was a costly one, and we lost General Huang Gai in the course of it. Because your brother had not a single inch of territory, we lent him Jingzhou as a base for his army. He has not yet returned it after all these years. Today I humbly beg to have Jingzhou back for a time to relieve our people. Once we have an ample reserve of grain, we may hand it back to you to govern. I

---

[35] 770-475 B.C.

shall not presume to decide on this matter. I hope Your Lordship will not take offence.

LORD:

Are you inviting me to a feast, or are you demanding Jingzhou?

LU:

No, no! Don't misunderstand me. Our rulers are bound by marriage. We desire to live at peace.

LORD:

> *You ought to be sincere when you play host,*
> *What is all this talk of the past?*
> *I have no patience with your high-flown phrases;*
> *Such a glib tongue should be cut off.*
> *You talk of our kingdoms' friendship,*
> *But treat us as enemies.*

LU:

So Your Lordship is overbearing and lacking in faith.

LORD:

Just why am I overbearing and lacking in faith?

LU:

Zhuge Liang himself promised that after Cao Cao was defeated he would return Jingzhou to us, and I acted as guarantor. But instead of remembering past obligations, today you have turned against us; yet you speak of requiting both the just and unjust. The sage said: When agreements are made in accordance with what is right, the words spoken can be made good. One can do without food or troops, but not without faith, any more than a carriage can do without a cross-bar. Now although you are so great a hero, Your Lordship, you have absolutely no sense of right. You have kept Jingzhou all this time, and refuse to return it. Yet a gentleman must keep faith.

LORD:

Lu Su, do you hear my sword clang?

LU:

What does it mean?

LORD:

The first time my sword clanged, I killed Wen Chou, the second time Cai Yang. Now I fear your turn has come.

LU:

No, no! You must not take it like that.

LORD:

To whom does Jingzhou belong?

LU:

Jingzhou is ours.

LORD:

You are wrong there. Listen to me.
Our first emperor built up the empire;
Emperor Guang Wu set right a wrong,
And Emperor Xian killed the usurper Dong Zhuo;
Liu Bei followed in their steps and killed Lu Bu,
So that the Han throne should be his.
What relationship has the King of Wu
To the royal house of Han'?
Answer me this, if you can, sir.

LU:

What is that sound?

LORD:

My sword has sounded for a second time.

LU:

What does it mean this time?

LORD:

This sword was forged with the spirit of the universe, the essence of fire and metal, the dual elements of nature, and the forms of the sun and the moon. Sheathed, it keeps ghosts away; unsheathed, it makes spirits scatter in fright. When it is happy, it rests still in the sheath; when it is angry, it leaps in its scabbard with a clang. There seems to be trouble brewing at your feast today. If you do not believe me I can show you my sword. Now I will sheathe it again. Don't lose your head.

This sword has irresistible might,
It is not a common weapon.
If you ask again for Jingzhou,
It will strike you dead at once.
For your wagging tongue
Has incensed my ruthless blade,
Which sups on generals' heads
And drinks the blood of foes.
It is a dragon hidden in its sheath,
A tiger couched between our seats;
We are meeting as old friends,
Let us have no quarrel.
Then listen well, Lu Su!
You have no cause for fear,
Set your mind at rest—
I am drunk.

LU:

Call for music, Zang Kong.
(Enter Zang Kong.)

ZANG:

There are five planets in heaven, five great mountains on earth, five virtues in men, and five notes in music. The five planets are those of gold, wood, water, fire and earth. The five mountains are Changshan, Hengshan, Taishan, Huashan and Songshan. The five virtues are gentleness, goodness, courtesy, frugality and

modesty. The five notes in music are *kong, shang, jiao, zhi* and *yii*.
(Enter Lu Su's Troops)

LU:

> Remain concealed, men!

LORD *(banging the table in rage)*:

> Is this an ambush?

LU:

> No, this is no ambush.

LORD:

> If it is, with one stroke I shall chop you into two!
> *(He smashes his fist on the table.)*

LU:

> You have broken the mirror.

LORD:

> I am here to make a break.
> *Why should your soldiery make such a noise?*
> *Mind they keep out of my way.*
> *If anyone crosses me—ha!*
> *He shall perish by my sword,*
> *His blood will spurt out!*
> *Even men as eloquent as Zhang Yi and Kuai Tong*[36]
> *Would do well not to waste their breath.*
> *Escort me instead to my boat,*
> *And I shall take a leisurely leave of you.*

LU:

> It will certainly be quieter if you leave.

HUANG:

> The ambush is ready, Your Honour.

---

[36] Famous orators.

LU:

It is too late now.
(Enter Guan Ping with his troops)

GUAN PING:

Father, please board your boat. We have come to meet you.

LORD:

I will trouble you to escort us, Lu Su.
I see my officers waiting
In purple robes and silver belts;
The evening breeze is cool,
The reeds are withering,
And my heart is well content.
Dark evening clouds are gathering,
The wind on the river is chill,
And sails flap in the breeze.
I thank you for your hospitality,
We are much obliged to you.
The boatman need not hurry;
Wait till the hawser is loosened.
Then let the prow cleave the waves,
And oars break the moon reflected in the water
Go slowly, for we are merry;
We shall laugh and chat all night.
There are two things I would remind you of:
You could not gain your end, for all your art;
For none shall overpower my loyal heart!
(THE END)

DEATH OF THE WINGED-TIGER GENERAL

CHARACTERS
Li Keyong's adopted sons
LI CUNXIN
KANGJUNLI
LI KEYONG, *a warlord at the end of the Tang Dynasty*
MADAM LIU, *his wife*
ZHOU DEWEI, *General of the Han and Tartar troops under Li Keyong*
LI CUNXIAO, *Li Keyong's adopted son, the Winged-Tiger General*
MADAM DENG, *Cunxiao's wife*
LANDLORD LI, *an old man*
BOY, *the landlord's adopted son*
MANGUTAI, *Madam Liu's maid*
TARTAR SOLDIERS

ACT I

(Enter Li Cunxin and Kang Junli.)

CUNXIN:

We gulp down pounds of mutton,
But cannot ride;
We know nothing of archery,
And cannot shoot.
At the sight of good wine
We start to swill,
Until we end up
In a drunken stupor.
Even our officers
Forget our names;
We are a pair of rogues,
A couple of curs.

邓夫人苦痛哭存孝杂剧

头折 冲末净李存信同康军刊上 李存信云 某

元 关汉卿

千整斤吞抹邓不会骑弓弯门开速门亏箭怎的射撒
因答刺孙见了抢着喫喝的莎塔八跌倒就是睡着
说我姓名家将不能记一对忽刺孩都是狗𩜙的自
记李存信的便是这个是亸刺俺两个不会开亏镫
号也不会厮杀相持哥：会唱我便能舞俺父亲是
子亢用阿妈喜欢俺两个无俺两个呵酒也不喫肉
也不喫若见俺两个呵便喫酒内好生的爱俺两个
目破黄巢之后太平无事阿妈复奪的城池地面着
俺百五义儿家将各处镇守阿妈的言语恃邢州与
邓夫人痛哭存孝

I am Li Cunxin and this is Kang Junli. We cannot draw a bow or fight, but he can sing and I can dance. We are the adopted sons of Li Keyong, who dotes on us. When we are away he takes neither meat nor wine, but when we are there he takes both—that shows how he loves us. Since Huang Chao[37] was defeated the empire has been at peace, and the old man has seized many cities and districts which are garrisoned by his five hundred adopted sons and officers. Now he has ordered us to garrison Xingzhou, but that is Zhu Wen's back door, and he is on bad terms with our father. When Zhu Wen knows we are there he will attack us, but we don't know how to fight—all we're good for is eating and drinking. What if he captures us and decides to kill us?

JUNLI:

The old man has made Cunxiao garrison commander of Luzhou, a place where you can enjoy good wine and good meat.. Let us prepare a farewell feast now for the old man. When we have made him drunk, we can tell him that Xingzhou is Zhu Wen's back door, and Zhu is on bad terms with father. If he attacks us it won't matter our being killed, but when others hear of it the old man's good name will suffer. So he had better let Cunxiao garrison Xingzhou.

CUNXIN:

Right, let's prepare a farewell feast. Come on!
I am Li Cunxin,
He is Kang Junli—
A pair of plausible
Rascals we! (Exeunt.)
(Enter Li Keyong and his wife Madam Liu, with Tartar Soldiers.)

LI:

Tartars! Tartars!

---

[37] Leader of a peasants' uprising towards the end of the Tang Dynasty (618-907 A.D.).

Wild country breeds rough fellows.
Thorough-bred horses,
Ornamented saddles,
Falcons and hounds,
Torrents and barren hills!
We slake our thirst with koumiss,
Our hunger with dried venison;
Our arrows have phoenix feathers,
Carved bows are slung on our arms;
Drunk in the forest
We whirl in Hunnish dances—
This is a truthful picture of Tartary. I am Li Keyong. I was once governor of Binzhou, but when I was drunk I beat Duan Wenchu, and was banished for ten years to Tartary. Then Huang Chao revolted, and the emperor made me commander-in-chief of the army of the northern provinces to suppress the rebels. Within a few days of leaving the steppes I reached the pass, and rallied the governors of twenty-four regions to win back the capital. My adopted son Cunxiao captured Deng Tianwang, brought back Meng Jiehai and killed Zhang Guiba. Then with eighteen horsemen he galloped to Chang-an, routed Huang Chao's army and regained the capital. By imperial decree my adopted sons and officers have been rewarded and given the towns they captured to garrison against the rebels. Now the empire is at peace. Quiet reigns within the four seas. I should drink and be merry with my wife and generals. Orderlies, prepare wine and food! Why is General Zhou Dewei not here yet? *(Enter Zhou Dewei.)*

ZHOU:

Twice the gong at headquarters has sounded;
Brave men are arrayed at the gate.
The troops raise a shout of greeting;
And the furled banners are still.

I am Zhou Dewei of Shuozhou. I helped Li Keyong to defeat Huang Chao, and now that the empire is at peace I have been appointed general of the Han and Tartar forces. Today the commander has summoned me to his headquarters. I must see what he wants. Here we are. *(To a Soldier.)* Announce my arrival, man.

SOLDIER:

Yes, sir. Commander Li, General Zhou is at the gate.

LI:

Ask him in.

SOLDIER:

Yes, sir. Please come in, General Zhou. *(Li and Zhou greet each other.)*

ZHOU:

Here I am, commander.

LI:

I'll tell you why I asked you here today, general. My adopted son Cunxiao has won such glory that I promised him Luzhou as his garrison area, and I want Cunxin and Junli to garrison Xingzhou. Why aren't they here yet?

(Enter Cunxin and Junli)

CUNXIN:

The old man thinks of us
And we arrive!
Don't worry, brother. When I get there and talk to the old man, he will send Cunxiao to Xingzhou.

JUNLI:

Watch your step, brother.

CUNXIN:

Father! Mother! Not long ago father promised to let us garrison Luzhou, but now you are giving it to Cunxiao and sending us to Xingzhou instead. *(He pretends to shed tears.)*

LI:

Why are you crying, son?

CUNXIN:

We have danced and sung day and night to keep you happy, father. Why should you send us to Xingzhou?

JUNLI:

Xingzhou is Zhu Wen's back door, father, and Zhu Wen is not on good terms with you. He may attack us, and we are no good at fighting. If he captures us we don't mind dying ourselves; but when you want us to sing and dance while you are drinking, and we aren't there, you may fall ill. Then you won't find us among all the herbs in the medicine shops.

CUNXIN:

Have a heart, father! Let us go to Luzhou and send Cunxiao and his wife to Xingzhou. How about it? *(He picks up a wine cup.)* Brother, bring the wine and we'll pour a cup for father.

LI:

What good sons you are! All right, you may go to Luzhou.

JUNLI:

Thank you, father!

ZHOU:

What have they done that they should go to Luzhou? Cunxiao the Winged-Tiger General fought up and down the country, slept in the saddle, and drank blood from his sword when thirsty. He should go to Luzhou, not they.

LI:

You are right, general. *(To a Soldier.)* Call Cunxiao and his wife.

SOLDIER:

Yes, commander. *(Enter Cunxiao and his wife.)*

CUNXIAO:

*I fought the tiger on the precipice,
Defeated the foe in battle*

292

And with my iron mace
Saved the house of Tang.

My name was An Jingsi. I am a native of Lingqiu near Swan Pass. My parents died when I was young, and Landlord Deng took me in and brought me up. I tended his sheep for him till my lord Li Keyong knew that I had killed a tiger and made me his officer and adopted son, giving me the titles of Winged Tiger and Thirteenth General. After that I married Deng's daughter. Since joining Li Keyong, I charged into Chang-an with eighteen horsemen and routed Huang Chao's army. Now that the empire is at peace, His Majesty has ordered us to garrison the towns and territory seized. My father has told me and my wife that we are to garrison Luzhou, and today he has sent for us. We must see what he wants. Here we are. Wait a moment before going in, ma'am. Look at our parents among all those flutes and drums, beef, horseflesh and abundance of delicacies, with five hundred Tartar boys and girls in attendance. Excellent!

DENG:

Yes, today they must want us to join them at a feast. Listen to that beautiful tune! They are making very merry.

Listen to the music played in unison!
He is descended from the house of Tang.
We come to pay respect to our step-parents—
Dragons and tigers met in wind and clouds.
On the great steppes of Tartary
Beauties in pearls and emeralds count as nothing,
Here are rare food and dainties,
Not just three paltry cups of watered wine.
Each day we dress the flesh of dragon and phoenix,
And slaughter sheep and horses for our feasts;
His adopted sons and retainers
Receive official posts as their reward,
Their sons and wives are granted ranks and titles.

Don't go over just yet, Cunxiao. Look at father—he has drunk too much already.

CUNXIAO:

Yes, he has spilt wine on his gown. See how they are holding him: he must be quite drunk.

DENG:

One is kneeling with cup and wine pot,
The other is making jokes.
Father does not care if his gown is stained with wine,
He helps himself absently,
Completely drunk.
Sweet music sounds beside him:
The roll of painted crocodile drums
And slow notes of cuckoo flutes.
See how smartly the troops are drawn up,
What pleasure he takes in wealth and nobility!
On one side sits General Zhou,
On the other Tartar officers serve food,
Between two ranks of soldiers.
Let us go over now.

CUNXIAO:

Very well, *(He greets Li.)* We have come, father.

LI:

So you have. My other sons have already gone to their posts. Today is an auspicious day. The two of you can set off to Xingzhou, while Junli and Cunxin start for Luzhou.

CUNXIAO:

Before we defeated Huang Chao, father, you promised that if we crushed the revolt and restored peace you would give me Luzhou. But now you are going back on your word. Today you tell me to garrison Xingzhou, which is Zhu Wen's back door, where I shall have to be fighting all the time. What does this mean?

DENG:

Let me ask mother to put in a word for us. Mother, please speak up for Cunxiao.

LIU:

You had better go to Xingzhou, son. Your father is drunk. You had better go.

CUNXIAO:

Father promised me Luzhou, but now he has more confidence in Junli and Cunxin and has ordered me to go to Xingzhou instead. Won't you speak to him for us, mother?

LIU:

Your father is drunk.

CUNXIAO:

Junli and Cunxin, what great deeds have you two done that you should go to Luzhou?

CUNXIN:

Father told you to go to Xingzhou. It's just as good. Who said anything about great deeds?

CUNXIAO:

When I stormed the citadel at Chang-an, there were three palisades, seven lines of defence, and a thousand of the enemy's best fighters drawn up in battle formation. But I trampled them under my feet as if they were nothing.

DENG:

> Our father is breaking his word.
> *Now the world is at peace you forget*
> *How when you needed men.*
> *Cunxiao quelled the rebels for you,*
> *How he battled so that you*
> *Might win fame and riches.*
> *Defences and palisades*
> *Were nothing to him.*
> *Despite their battle formations,*
> *Fierce generals and cunning strategy,*
> *He preserved the great Tang empire.*

CUNXIAO:

You, Junli and Cunxin! What great deeds have you done that you should go to Luzhou?

DENG:

He never unbuckled his armour,
His horse was never unsaddled.
Mother should remind our father
Of all Cunxiao did for them.
Why should men with no feats to their credit
Receive good cities
While Cunxiao goes unrewarded?

LIU:

Your father is drunk, child. We will speak to him again when he is sober.

DENG:

But what have Junli and Cunxin done?
You two fellows are nothing but gluttons
Who let others fight the fierce battles
And never consider the hardships that they have suffered.
Father, you are favouring Cunxin and Junli.
Remember how Cunxiao fought with his horse and lance!
Now you are letting him down
And treating your sons unjustly.

CUNXIAO:

Junli and Cunxin, I charged into the capital with eighteen horsemen, defeated Ge Congzhou, routed Huang Chao and restored peace. That was my work—what have you done?

CUNXIN:

We have never distinguished ourselves in battle, but we can sing and dance.

DENG:

While he rode back victorious

With songs of triumph,
Smiling as he beat his golden stirrup with his whip,
And saw his embroidered standard float in the wind,
You were trembling,
Scared out of your wits,
Running away as fast as you could from the battle.

CUNXIAO:

What have you two to your credit? Can you ride a spirited horse, or bend a strong bow? All you can do is gorge meat and wine. That is all you are fit for.

DENG:

Can you ride a spirited horse
Or bend a strong bow?
While he covered himself with glory in the field,
You lounged in camp.
This is the truth—
You need not try to deceive us.
Hungry, you clamour for meat;
Thirsty, you look for koumiss;
To pass the time you dice,
And once you are drunk
What ludicrous songs you sing.
You cannot handle one of the eighteen weapons,
You cannot wield mace or club,
And you will not bare your arms
To fight with a sword;
When horses neigh
In the bustle and din of the camp,
You nearly die of fright.

Cunxiao, today is an auspicious day. Let us collect our baggage and horses, say goodbye to our parents and set off on our long journey.

CUNXIAO:

Yes, today is an auspicious day. Let us say goodbye to our parents and set off on our long journey.

DENG:

> Say no more.
> *Your brothers are no true brothers to you,*
> *And now I have offended our parents.*

LIU:

> Don't be so impatient, child. When your father wakes up, we can discuss this again.

DENG:

> No, we must be going.
> *You need reproach us no more;*
> *After all, we were not born in the house of Li.*
> *May Heaven see this injustice!*
> *It is lucky—*
> *That we shall be far apart,*
> *Each in our own city,*
> *Otherwise Cunxin and Junli*
> *Would be in for trouble—*
> *One a downright liar,*
> *The other a fawning flatterer,*
> *Two glib, deceitful knaves!*
> *(Exeunt Cunxiao and Madam Deng.)*

LIU:

> Junli and Cunxin, your father is drunk. I will take him inside.
> *(Exeunt Madam Liu and Li)*

ZHOU:

> Cunxiao defeated Huang Chao and re-established the Tang empire, yet his good land has been given to these two, while he gets Xingzhou. Today the commander is drunk. Tomorrow when he is sober I must speak to him, and persuade him to send Cunxiao and his wife to Luzhou. Nothing less will satisfy me.
> *The drunken commander has wronged Cunxiao.*
> *Tomorrow we must set this injustice right. (Exit.)*

CUNXIN:

Well, Junli, what do you say now? I told you we'd get Luzhou, and you see I was right. Going to a rich place like that will be better than being in Xingzhou and fighting every day with Zhu Wen's men.

JUNLI:

But now Cunxiao bears a grudge against us, brother. Once we get to Luzhou we must accuse him of some fault so that the old man has him killed. That's the only way we'll be safe. I tell you what—let's pack up today and go to Xingzhou. Then we can pretend that we have orders from the old man that all his adopted sons and retainers are to use their own names again; and once Cunxiao uses his old name, we can accuse him and have him killed. Then our greatest wish will be granted.

The old man is fond of drinking,
Once drunk he is like a swine;
We are going to kill An Jingsi
To have our own way. (Exeunt)

ACT II

(Enter Cunxiao with Tartar Troops.)

CUNXIAO:

In shining helmet and close-fitting habit,
A tiger-skin above my new silk robe,
I have won great fame in battle,
And garrison Xingzhou to protect the people.

I am Li Cunxiao the Thirteenth General, formerly I was commander of the vanguard, conqueror of Huang Chao, and halberdier-general. Since coming to govern Xingzhou, I have trained my troops well and governed with justice. I have defeated Wang Yanzhang, who dared not look me in the face, and kept Zhu Wen from invading our territory. Today I have no business. I am sitting in my office to see if anyone comes.

(Enter Cunxin and Junli.)

CUNXIN:

From Luzhou we come to Xingzhou;
I am Cunxin, he is Junli.

Here we are. This is the Xingzhou office. Go in, fellow, and report that Li Cunxin and Kang Junli are at the gate.

SOLDIER:

Yes, sir. *(Announcing them.)* General Li! Li Cunxin and Kang Junli are here.

CUNXIAO:

So my brothers have come. They must have brought orders from our father. Ask them in.

SOLDIER:

Yes, sir. Please come in.
(Cunxin and Junli greet Cunxiao)

JUNLI:

Cunxiao, this is our father's order. You have done many great deeds and he fears your own family name may be forgotten, so he orders you to give up the surname Li and take the name of An Jingsi again. If you disobey him, he will have you killed. You had better make the change at once. We must leave now to report back to our father.

CUNXIAO:

Why should he want me to change my name? Still, this is my father's order, and I dare not disobey. Men, prepare a feast for my brothers.

JUNLI:

We won't stop to eat. We must go back to the old man.
We have given him a false order
To make him change his name;
The old man will be angry,
Then off with his head!
And all will be well for us!
(Exeunt Junli and Cunxin.)

CUNXIAO:

Ah, father, it was you who helped me win my present rank with a wife and son to share my high position. Why do you want me to change my name now? I fought hard, endured frost and snow, and distinguished myself in battle; but today you cast me off.
He is drunk every day,
He listens to liars and injures honest men.
I am Cunxiao who pacified the land,
But now there is peace the veteran is not wanted. (Exit.)
(Enter Li Keyong and Madam Liu.)

LI:

Happy days of peace and quiet—
Time to feast with silk-clad girls.
I am Li Keyong. By imperial decree my adopted sons and retainers are garrisoning different parts of the empire. The whole world is at peace—we can drink and be merry. Let us see who is coming here. *(Enter Cunxin and Junli.)*

JUNLI:

    Father, trouble has started!

LI:

    What is the matter now?

JUNLI:

    After Cunxiao went to Xingzhou, because he was angry with you for not giving him Luzhou he changed his name to An Jingsi, and means to lead his Winged-Tiger Army against you. What shall we do?

CUNXIN:

    If he kills you, what will become of us, father?

LI:

    How dare Cunxiao do such a thing? He could change his name, but why lead an army against me? I won't let him off lightly. Today I shall mobilize my Tartar troops and arrest that shepherd myself.

LIU:

    Wait a bit, commander. Why not think this over? Young Cunxiao would never do a thing like that, you can be sure. Let me first go to Xingzhou. If he has not changed his name, well and good. If he has, we can still mobilize our troops to capture him.

    We need no swordsmen, halberdiers,
    Or lancers to show our might;
    I shall make use of cunning
    And deliver Cunxiao to you with my bare hands. (Exit.)

LI:

    Junli and Cunxin, your mother has already gone there. If she finds Cunxiao has really revolted, I shall go myself to catch that shepherd boy. Tell my brave officers and men to make ready.

    Put on your helmets and armour,
    Fit arrows to your bows,
    Shoulder your lances and halberds,

Brandish your swords and sabres.
Our vanguard, three thousand strong,
Will cross the mountains and streams;
My left troops are skilled soldiers,
My right troops are fierce and brave,
My rearguard will bring up supplies,
And my five hundred retainers
Will fight like heroes in front.
Our chargers are fierce as dragons,
Our officers brave as tigers;
I shall lead my men to Xingzhou
To seize that ungrateful cub.
My men are seasoned campaigners,
My Tartar officers are brave and daring;
I shall kill him with my own hands,
Splashing the blood over the eastern sky! (Exeunt.)
(Enter Cunxiao with his wife and soldiers)

CUNXIAO:

Before we Can enjoy happiness, fresh trouble has started, ma'am. My father has told Junli and Cunxin to inform me that his five hundred adopted sons and retainers are ordered to change their names. I am to give up the name of Li and call myself An Jingsi again. It seems to me our father puts too much trust in that couple. What shall we do?

DENG:

You had better not believe those two scoundrels, my lord. Be careful that you don't fall into a trap.

CUNXIAO:

It was they who came to order me to change my name. It is not that I want to change it.

DENG:

If your father has ordered you to change, you must. But govern loyally and show the people justice,
The proverb says:

Good magistrates make happy people;
Just laws are pleasing to Heaven;
Poor families may have filial sons;
Let us do what good we can.
If our father orders us to change our name,
We need not stamp with rage;
Today he fancies we disgrace his house,
But there was a time when he wanted you for his son.

CUNXIAO:

When we were fighting Huang Chao, ma'am, he made me his son and a member of his family. He would have done better not to adopt me then.

DENG:

We relied not on powerful friends,
Nor on family connections.
We fought Huang Chao
In three thousand bloody battles,
Braved many dangers and hardships,
And at last gained official rank,
Both wife and sons sharing the honour.
Before we reached high estate
And lived in painted halls,
Before we governed the people in this office,
We conquered and captured foes...
But now he doubts our loyalty,
Believes wicked lies about us,
Doubts a filial son
And puts trust in heartless rogues,
Unable to distinguish good from evil.

CUNXIAO:

Let us wait here, ma'am. *(To a Soldier.)* Go and see who is outside. *(Enter an Old Man with a Boy.)*

OLD MAN:

I am Landlord Li. Because I had no son I adopted this boy. Now I have land, a fine house and farm tools, as well as a son of my own. I don't need you now. Get out.

BOY:

Father, when you had no son of your own, I became your son. But now that you have land, a house and farm tools, you don't want me. Here is a good official. Let us ask him to decide between us. Here we are at the office. Justice!

CUNXIAO:

Who is that shouting at the gate? Bring him in.

SOLDIER *(bringing them forward):*

Here they are, sir.
(The Old Man and the Boy kneel before Cunxiao.)

CUNXIAO:

Well, boy, what is your complaint?

BOY:

Mercy, Your Honour! When my father had no son he adopted me. But now that he has land, a house and farm tools, as well as a son of his own, he has no further use for me and wants to drive me out. So I come to appeal to you. Have mercy, and decide between us!

CUNXIAO:

This boy's fate is like mine. In time of need, my father had a use for me; but now he has other sons he casts me off. Guards, beat that old man!

DENG:

Wait! Don't beat him.
I listen with sinking heart,
It is not right
To beat this foolish old man.

> *If father and son have quarrelled*
> *That is only natural.*

CUNXIAO:

Guards, beat that man!

DENG:

> *You condemn him unheard,*
> *You beat him before he can speak;*
> *What a wrong-headed judge you are!*
> *Oh, you will kill him!*
> *And what rough guards you have!*

CUNXIAO:

Drive him out.

SOLDIER:

Yes, sir. Get out!

OLD MAN:

So I have been beaten for nothing. I shall lodge a complaint somewhere else.
(Exeunt.)
(Enter Madam Liu.)

LIU:

I am Li Keyong's wife, Madam Liu. Hearing that Cunxiao has changed his family name, I have come post-haste to Xingzhou. When I made inquiries, I found it was true that he calls himself An Jingsi now. Here is Cunxiao's house.

Go and announce me, fellow.

SOLDIER:

Yes, ma'am. Your Excellency, Madam Liu is here.

DENG:

Go and welcome mother while I change my clothes.
(She steps aside and changes her clothes)

CUNXIAO *(greeting Madam Liu):*

If I had known you were coming, mother, I should have gone to welcome you. Forgive me for failing in respect. *(He bows.)*

LIU *(angrily):*

Cunxiao, what wrong has your father done you? Why should you change your name? How could you do such a thing?

CUNXIAO:

Please don't be angry, mother. Men, prepare wine and sweetmeats.

SOLDIER:

Yes, sir.

CUNXIAO *(presenting wine):*

Mother, please drink this cup.

LIU:

No, Cunxiao, I will not drink.

DENG:

I won't go to her yet but watch from here. Mother seems rather upset. I wonder why?
I saw her alight from her horse and enter the gate,
Walking slowly up the steps.
I see Cunxiao with cup and wine pot,
But she will not touch a drop.
I see how angry she looks,
Refusing to be appeased.
Standing humbly on one side
I dare not show any lack of due respect,
But curtsey and advance with folded hands—
Did you have a good journey, mother?

LIU:

Please excuse me for disturbing you, Madam An Jingsi.

DENG:
>This is most disquieting!
>*Now I know why she is angry,*
>*And need not ask the reason.*
>*But we can explain what happened.*

LIU:
>Child, have we two old people done you any wrong? Why should you change your name? If Junli and Cunxin had not told us, we should not even have known. Your father wanted to bring Tartar troops to arrest you, but I could not believe it was true so I came myself. However, I find you really have changed your name. Tell me what wrong we have done you.

DENG:
>Cunxiao, now is the time to speak.

CUNXIAO:
>Mother, it was Kang Junli and Li Cunxin who told me that our father had ordered all his five hundred adopted sons and retainers to change their names and made me take the name of An again. It was you, father and mother, who helped me reach my present position, win noble titles for my wife and son, and occupy such a high official post. How could I ever forget your kindness?
>*(He weeps)*
>*I cannot help shedding tears;*
>*My heart is racked with pain.*
>*You raised me to high estate and fame,*
>*How could I forget my adopted father and mother?*

LIU:
>So you did not do this yourself. In that case your father has no reason to be angry.

DENG:
>*As vanguard commander*
>*He strove with all his might,*
>*Exerting his strength and courage to the utmost,*

> *Galloping with silken standard*
> *To storm the enemy's camp.*
> *He won glory for you, mother,*
> *Restored the empire and routed Huang Chao for you,*
> *Fought Zhang Guiba and defeated Zhu Wen.*
> *In those days you welcomed his talents,*
> *But now we have laid down arms—*
> *No more battles, soldiers, horses and frontier alarms—*
> *You have forgotten us!*
> *In time of peace you no longer need your general.*
> *Hundreds of battles just for a scrap of paper—*
> *But the dead are forgotten now in their high tombs.*

LIU:

Stay here, daughter, while I go with Cunxiao to his father to expose those two scoundrels' lies.

DENG:

Don't take him with you, mother. If Junli and Cunxin are there, he will lose his life for nothing.

LIU:

Set your mind at rest, child. We must clear up this slander. Wait here while I take Cunxiao with me. I know what to do.

CUNXIAO:

This time I must clear myself. Don't worry, ma'am.

DENG:

> *Let mother clear up the trouble,*
> *Or father will still be angry.*
> *We count on the god of luck*
> *To distinguish true from false*
> *And root up the source of our calamity.*
> *Use those fists that have killed tigers*
> *To pound Junli and Cunxin*
> *Till they confess their crime*
> *Of seizing Luzhou from you,*

And we are avenged. (Exit.)

LIU:

Pack up your luggage, son, and come with me to your father.
We can see to the bottom of deep pools;
Only the human heart is hard to fathom.
(Exeunt.)
(Enter Li Keyong, Cunxin and Junli)

LI:

Junli and Cunxin, since your mother left we have heard nothing to confirm that rumour. Bring me wine. Weren't you mistaken about Cunxiao?

CUNXIN:

He *has* changed his name, father. How dare I lie to you?

JUNLI:

If we lied, may a big gust of wind blow my hat away!

LI:

So it is true. Bring me wine. I'll drink a few cups.

JUNLI:

A good idea. Yes, drink a few cups.
(Enter Liu and Cunxiao.)

LIU:

Here we are, son. *(To the Guard)* Go in, man, and announce me.

LI:

So she is back. Ask her to come in to drink a few cups.

GUARD:

Yes, sir. Please come in, ma'am.

CUNXIAO:

Go in first and say a good word for me, mother.

311

LIU:

Don't worry, son. I will. *(She greets Li.)* So you are drunk again, husband. If I hadn't gone, you would have done Cunxiao a serious wrong.

CUNXIN:

Mother! Brother Yazi has been thrown from his horse in the hunt.

LIU *(alarmed):*

What's that? I must go to my son!

CUNXIAO *(seizing her sleeve):*

Put in a good word for me, mother!

LIU:

My son Yazi has been thrown in the hunt. I must go and see him. I shall come back very soon.

CUNXIAO:

You are leaving me, mother, and my father is drunk. He will listen to those two villains and have me killed.

LIU:

Can't you understand? My own son has fallen from his horse and been killed. How can a mother behave as if nothing had happened? He is my own flesh and blood. I cannot look after you now—I must go to my son. *(She pushes him aside and goes out.)*

CUNXIAO *(shedding tears):*

Ah, mother!
Yazi has been thrown
And she is broken-hearted,
For they are one flesh and blood.
When the choice lies between
An adopted son and her own,
The difference is clear as noonday.
Yazi was flesh of her flesh,

While I am a stranger.
She mourns for her own:
Her own child is more dear to her.

CUNXIN *(offering wine):*

Father, drink one more cup.

LI *(reeling):*

I am drunk.

JUNLI:

Cunxiao is at the gate, father. He is disloyal and ungrateful.

LI:

I feel distempered. *(Exit.)*

CUNXIN:

The old man said he felt distempered, brother. He is drunk. What shall we do? Suppose tomorrow when he wakes up, we say that he told us to have Cunxiao dismembered?

JUNLI:

Right! If we don't kill him, tomorrow when the old man wakes up and listens to his wife, we shall die. Men, arrest Cunxiao!

CUNXIAO:

Where are you taking me, Cunxin and Junli?

CUNXIN:

These are our father's orders. For your ingratitude and disloyalty, you are to be torn to pieces by five carts.

CUNXIAO:

Cruel father! What wrong have I done that I should be torn to pieces? I shall die here while my wife at home does not know I am dead. Brothers An Xiuxiu and Xue Atan, send my tiger-skin robe and turban and my iron mace to her. This is my last gift to her. *(Weeping.)* Ah, wife!

*Today I shall perish here,
I am on my way to the execution ground.
My wife will lose her husband,
My heart is broken as I think of our love.
Withered grass-blades on the misty plain
Will be my companions,
Dead trees and desolate tombs
Will be my home;
Only in her dreams
Shall we ever meet again.*

CUNXIN:

Just listen to me!
*We laid our plans with cunning
To hasten the shepherd boy's death;
You fell into our trap and changed your name,
Now we have got you from Xingzhou to have you killed!*

CUNXIAO:

As Heaven is my witness, I have served the Li family and the empire well. I captured Meng Jiehai alive; in my rage I seized Deng Tianwang, defeated Zhang Guiba, stormed Taiyuan and took back Bingzhou, killing five enemy commanders. In the great battle of Huayanchuan, I defeated Ge Congzhou; then with eighteen horsemen I charged into Chang-an and routed Huang Chao, restoring the Tang empire. These are my achievements. Today I am not needed, and you want to have me dismembered. *(He sheds tears)* Enough!

*My high ambitions towered to the stars,
Heaven decreed me a noble.
I risked my life to prop the tottering throne,
And fought hard at the head of the spearmen.
Flags gleamed in the sun like serpents;
Now wild flowers bloom over sad battlefields,
The hero is wrongly killed—
This is the fruit of loyalty and goodness!*
Ah, wife, I am dying of bitterness! *(Exit.)*

CUNXIN:

Today we will have him torn limb from limb. When the old man questions us tomorrow, we can think of some answer. Come on.

The cicada knows when autumn is at hand,
But death comes stealthily and unforeseen.
(Exeunt)
(Enter Zhou Dewei)

ZHOU:

Events may surprise us, but there is a reason for all things. I am Zhou Dewei. This is a fearful business—Li Keyong while drunk has had Cunxiao killed. Taken in by Junli and Cunxin's lies, he had the Tiger General dismembered. Yesterday he was in a drunken stupor. I am on my way now to his headquarters to find out exactly what happened.

Two scoundrels plotted together
And had Cunxiao dismembered.
Now Tartar officers are crowding his tent—
Let us see what Li has to say! (Exit.)

ACT III

(Enter Madam Liu.)

LIU:

I never learned needlework or embroidery,
With bent bow on horseback I fight the enemy;
I shoot tigers with the hunters,
And know stratagems of war.

I am Madam Liu. Yesterday I brought Cunxiao to see his father, but just as I was going to explain matters I heard that my son Yazi had been thrown while hunting. When I hurried to see him, I found nothing had happened—it was a trick played by Cunxin and Junli. I wonder what has happened to Cunxiao. I have sent a messenger to find out. She should be back by now. *(Enter Mangutai)*

MANGUTAI:

I am Mangutai. Our mistress told me to find out what happened to Cunxiao. It seems that when the master was drunk he believed Junli and Cunxin, and had Cunxiao dismembered. I dare not delay, but must report this at once.

Two treacherous villains
Were treated as loyal men
By our heartless, drunken master.
Those two are like vipers and scorpions:
Their hearts are evil.
I move as fast as a windmill
To hurry back to the house,
Running the whole way,
Giving my feet no rest.
I shall tell our lady the truth from the beginning.
It is done, the water is spilt,
The dead cannot speak;
There is no remedy now.

LIU:

What a fine young Tartar!

> With well-fitted cap and sable coat,
> She runs as if she had wings.
> She will give me news of Cunxiao,
> And tell me the truth of the matter.

Well, you must have seen Cunxiao. His father was drunk—what did Junli and Cunxin say to him? When you are less out of breath, tell me all that happened.

MANGUTAI:

> Our master has no sense when he is drunk,
> Junli and Cunxin wagged their tongues,
> Shook their heads,
> And slandered the hero.
> They gave him no chance to answer,
> But worked hand in glove to destroy him.

LIU:

What did your master say, girl? What did Cunxiao say?
> My husband was drunk;
> Cunxiao is good and loyal;
> Son and father loved each other
> Till Cunxin and Junli made trouble.

What words did your master have with Cunxiao, tell me that.

MANGUTAI:

> One was a good son,
> The other a good father,
> But their love was destroyed by others.
> An evil influence on the father's side
> Made him unkind to his son;
> And slanderers said:
> "How can a son of An be an heir of Li?"

LIU:

Do you know that there were two traitors with your master, girl?

MANGUTAI:
>Who were they?

LIU:
>*Kang Junli, that two-tailed scorpion,*
>*Li Cunxin, that double-faced snake.*
>*With no loyalty to the state*
>*They plotted to harm the hero.*
>How did those two men argue their case?

MANGUTAI:
>I will tell you all, ma'am, if you can bear to hear it.
>*Junli is a savage wolf,*
>*Cunxin a poisonous snake;*
>*Their dastardly deed*
>*Was something unheard of before.*
>*Cunxiao's loyalty was vain;*
>*Our master is fickle.*

LIU:
>*My son Cunxiao risked his life at Huayanchuan*
>*To defeat Huang Chao and pacify the state.*
>*He was the fade pillar supporting the vault of heaven,*
>*The golden bridge spanning the ocean.*
>What did those two scoundrels do to him?

MANGUTAI:
>*The golden bridge was broken:*
>How could he defend himself, ma'am?
>*Once he charged with eighteen horsemen into Chang-an,*
>*Now he is only a spirit riding the wind—*
>It's enough to break your heart.
>*You will no more see him again*
>*Than catch the moon in a pool.*

LIU:
>What are you keeping back, girl?

MANGUTAI:

    Thanks to Cunxin and Junli, Cunxiao was torn to pieces by five carts.

LIU:

> Ah, my unhappy child!
> *They must have beaten him*
> *And cursed him again and again!*
> *His spirit has gone to the shades*
> *With unavenged wrongs.*
> How did he meet his death?

MANGUTAI:

> *With a shout like a thunderbolt,*
> *Like a cruel hawk catching a dove,*
> *The pair rushed forward.*
> *They gave Cunxiao no chance to speak.*
> *One abused him thirty times,*
> *The other kicked him six times in the ribs.*
> *It was a fearful sight!*
> *He was torn limb from limb,*
> *Torn to pieces by the carts!*

LIU:

    Did they try to extract a confession from him before they took the hero to the execution ground and murdered him?

MANGUTAI:

> *They did not ask him to confess,*
> *Nor did they sign a warrant for his execution.*
> *He was pushed away,*
> *With soldiers around him like iron hoops,*
> *With a forest of clubs before and behind,*
> *He was dragged to the execution ground.*
> *Two scoundrels had their wish,*
> *And one gallant man was murdered.*

LIU:

Think of all my son Cunxiao did for the country! He captured Meng Jiehai alive, killed Deng Tianwang, pierced Zhang Guiba with his lance, and charged with eighteen steeds into Chang-an. He killed Geng Biao with his mace, and burned the Yongfeng Granary. He had the strength of nine bulls and could kill a tiger. How did he meet his death?

MANGUTAI:

Cunxiao said:
I killed Deng Tianwang beneath his flag,
Dragged Meng Jiehai from his horse,
Beat a tiger till it streamed with blood,
And killed a thousand men with my two maces.
But today the strength of nine bulls
Cannot withstand five carts.
The general died in agony,
All that saw it were appalled.

LIU:

When the five carts with five times five bulls started pulling, what then?

MANGUTAI:

They beat the bulls to make them jump with fright,
Shouted to urge them on;
Whips cracked and the bulls strained together,
So the Winged-Tiger General was killed. (Exit.)

LIU:

Cruel Keyong! You believed two lying scoundrels and had Cunxiao killed so unjustly.
Five carts pulled in five directions—
Even a man of iron would utter a cry.
Bone and flesh were torn apart,
His blood stained the yellow sand.
Never again shall I see my son—
The thought of it breaks my heart.

*I am bowed with sorrow,
And Cunxiao has gone to the shades. (Weeps.)*
Ah, Cunxiao, my son, your mother will die of grief! *(Exit.)*

ACT IV

(Enter Li Keyong, Cunxin, Junli and Tartar Troops.)

LI:

Shepherd pipes flute in the wilderness,
A north wind blows, chargers neigh.
We beat painted drums inlaid with gold,
Black banners flutter against the clouds and the moon.

I am Li Keyong. Yesterday I made merry with my officers till I was drunk. They say that Cunxiao is here. Scout, bring Cunxiao to me.

CUNXIN:

Now what shall we do?
(Enter Madam Liu.)

LIU:

A fine thing you have done, Li Keyong! How could you listen to those two scoundrels who make you drunk every day, and have Cunxiao dismembered? I went to Xingzhou myself to find out the truth, and discovered that he did not change his name: it was those devils Cunxin and Junli who tricked him into calling himself An Jingsi. Yesterday I brought Cunxiao to see you. How could you let those wicked men dismember him? His wife has taken his bones to Deng Village. Ah, you have broken my heart!

LI:

Madam, I knew nothing of this. It was all their doing. I said that I felt distempered because I was drunk—how dare they have him dismembered! Let those two wicked men be taken to Deng Village and killed. Let their bellies be opened and their hearts taken out, to avenge my son. Have a shrine and sacrifice prepared, and let someone fetch Cunxiao's wife. *(He sheds tears)* Ah, Cunxiao, my son, my son!

My tears stream down,
My heart seems pierced with a sword,
Ml my adopted sons and retainers mourn,

> Because in my cups I killed a loyal man-It was Cunxin and Junli, the scoundrels,
> Who had Cunxiao dismembered.
> Let all my sons put on mourning,
> Let my Tartar officers and men lament.
> Alas, my good and loyal son,
> Do not think too harshly of your faithless parents! *(Exeunt.)*
> *(Enter Madam Deng carrying the pennant to call the dead man's spirit.)*

DENG:

> Ah, Cunxiao, my heart is broken.
> *I wave the pennant from side to side—*
> *Your spirit must not lose its way!*
> *My tears stream unceasingly,*
> *My heart is burning with anguish.*
> *No matter how long the road,*
> *I shall reach my goal in the end.*
> I wave the pennant,
> I carry the box with your ashes on my back.
> Your spirit flies on high—where is it now?
> Surely this is Winged-Tiger Valley?
> *You must not miss the place and pass us by.*
> *I cannot stop sobbing with anguish,*
> *Faint with sorrow. Oh, Heaven!*
> *My heart is racked with pain! (Enter Madam Liu)*

LIU:

> Isn't that my daughter-in-law? Let me call her to make sure. Madam Deng! Daughter! Wait a moment.

DENG:

> *I hasten on without a pause.*
> *Who is that calling me?*

LIU:

> Madam Deng, it is I! *(She greets her and weeps)* Alas, Cunxiao, sorrow will carry me to my grave.

DENG:
> *Mother, you caused my husband's death.*

LIU:
> What did I do?

DENG:
> *You promised that all would be well,*
> *That the misunderstanding would be explained away.*

LIU:
> Ah, daughter, not a word have you forgotten.

DENG:
> *My heart is bursting,*
> *But to whom can I speak?*

LIU:
> Child, put down the box with his remains. Your father is bringing those two scoundrels here to avenge Cunxiao.
> *(Enter Li Keyong, Zhou Dewei and Tartar Troops escorting Cunxin and Junli in chains.)*

LI:
> I am to blame for this, daughter. You need not be afraid to reproach me. Now bring the sacrificial objects. Put the tiger-skin turban, the tiger-belt and the iron maces before the shrine. Let Kang Junli and Li Cunxin be tied up and brought here. Those wicked men shall die a lingering death. Now General Zhou will read the funeral speech.

ZHOU *(reading):*
> On the tenth of the ninth month of the first year of Qianning[38] of the Tang Dynasty, Li Keyong, commander-in-chief of the northern provinces and conqueror of Huang Chao, offers

---

[38] A.D. 894.

sacrifice with his generals before the shrine of his late adopted son, Li Cunxiao the Winged-Tiger General. Here is the dirge: "Reared in the northern steppes, you spent your youth in Winged-Tiger Valley and fought countless battles against the enemy. You were skilled in the use of the bow, and could shoot both right and left. You were invincible when you wielded your maces, and could fell an opponent with a single blow. You overcame a tiger in the mountains and routed the rebels in the capital. You struck Geng Biao dead with your mace, killed the three commanders and the five tiger generals, smashed the enemy's serpent formation and defeated Ge Congzhou. Then you fought three battles at Weinan, and with eighteen horsemen galloped into the capital. You shot Huang Juyao, fought Fu Cunshen, vanquished Li Hanzhi, and captured Deng Tianwang. You beat Gao Siji during an illness, caught Meng Jiehai and routed Wang Yanzhang. Then you entered Chang-an a second time so that the people might live in peace again. But I, Li Keyong, after drinking listened to slander and wronged my adopted son. I shall execute these murderers now to avenge you, and all my generals shall mourn for you.

> *We wail till the grass and trees,*
> *Green hills, earth and sky turn pale.*
> *No more will you wear the commander's golden seal,*
> *But, a shade, will command ghostly troops.*
> *The Tartar officers mourn with their men,*
> *Your maces hanging here bear blood-stains still,*
> *Your charger in the court misses its master;*
> *Your tiger robe hangs limp before your tent.*
> *Brave Cunxiao is no more.*
> *He achieved many deeds of valour,*
> *He served the state loyally.*
> *And gave peace to the empire;*
> *His name will live for all eternity.*
> *May your spirit come to the sacrifice!"*

DENG:

> *His father has admitted wronging him,*
> *His comrades-in-arms are wailing bitterly;*

> *Recalling his mighty deeds and immortal fame,*
> *They have put on mourning for him*
> *And are kneeling before the shrine.*
> *Alas, your achievements were vain—*
> *Quiet hang the two iron maces,*
> *The bright embroidered flag flutters in the wind,*
> *The painted drum sounds and the bugle.*
> *In tiger-skin turban*
> *On bay charger,*
> *hearing steel-tipped arrows*
> *And bow with painted tassels,*
> *You stayed in frosty tents in ice-bound country*
> *Where battles raged and enemy forces swarmed.*
> *Seeing these relics now,*
> *My heart bleeds for you, Cunxiao.*
> *The tiger-skin robe hangs limp before your tent,*
> *In vain you risked death to restore the house of Tang,*
> *Or galloped across the bridge with lance in hand—*
> *This is the end!*
> *In vain you routed Huang Chao with eighteen horsemen.*

LI:

Take Cunxin and Junli to the shrine, men, and have them killed.

SOLDIERS *(seizing them):*

Yes, sir!

CUNXIN:

Have pity, father! Spare us!

JUNLI:

If you spare us this time, father, we won't do it again.

DENG:

> *Junli and Cunxin,*
> *You brought this on yourselves,*
> *You murdered Cunxiao,*

And destroyed my family;
You shall not escape retribution,
But receive your due deserts.
You should be sliced and pounded,
The crowd clamours for your blood!
Get carts and horses ready,
And ropes to tie them up,
Then have them torn to pieces
So that Cunxiao is avenged!

LI:

Have the villains dismembered, men!
(The soldiers shout their assent, making ready to kill them.)

CUNXIN:

It's all up with us.
(Exeunt.)

LI:

Now that the murderers are being torn limb from limb, my son Cunxiao is avenged. Let posthumous honours be granted at his grave, and you, Madam Deng, shall have a good city to support your old age. Mark what I say:
Li Cunxin envied an able man,
And the Winged-Tiger General was unjustly accused.
His wife is stricken with grief,
Bowed down by her husband's death.
Now wicked Junli and Cunxin
Have been torn apart by five carts in the public square,
We shall hold a grand sacrifice
To send Cunxiao's spirit to Heaven.
(THE END)